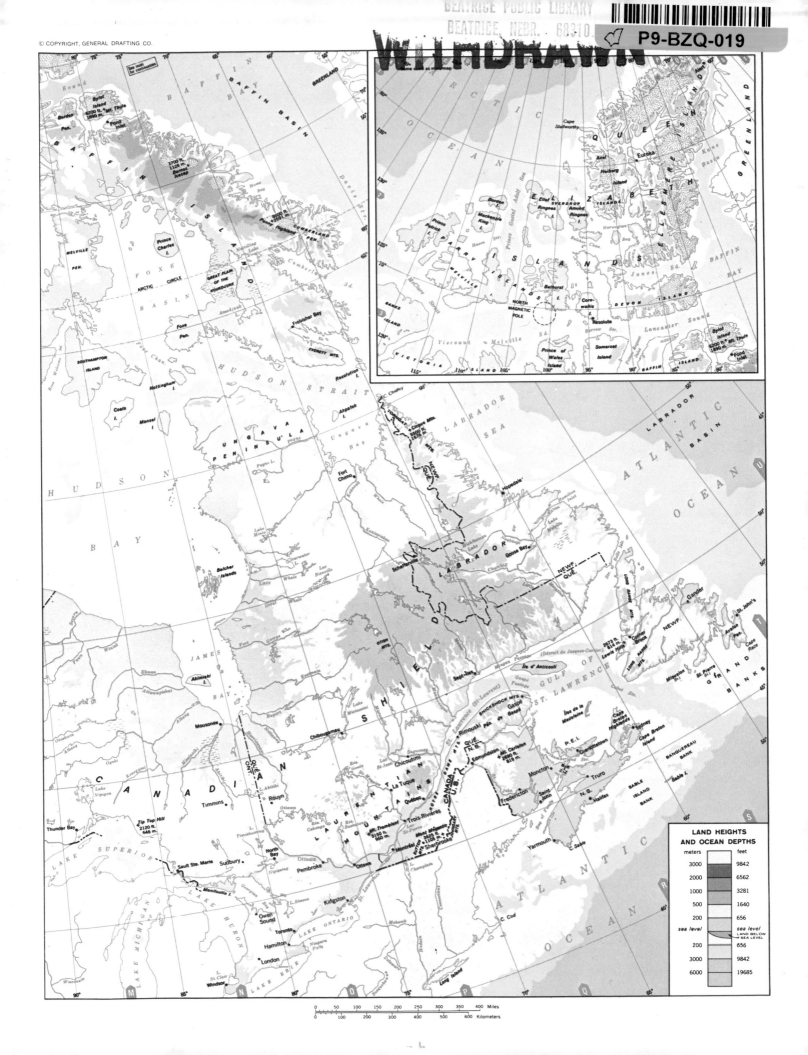

LAND HEIGHTS
AND OCEAN DEPTHS

meters	feet
3000	9842
2000	6562
1000	3281
500	1640
200	656
sea level	sea level
	LAND BELOW SEA LEVEL
200	656
3000	9842
6000	19685

0 50 100 150 200 250 300 350 400 Miles
0 100 200 300 400 500 600 Kilometers

Ontario

ANTHONY HOCKING

Publisher: John A. Savage

Managing Editor: Robin Brass

Research Editor: Rosemary Aubert

Manuscript Editor: Jocelyn Van Huyse

Production Supervisor: Rachel Mansfield

Design: Tibor Kovalik

Graphics: Pirjo Selistemagi

Cover: Veronica Hill

◫THE CANADA SERIES

McGRAW-HILL RYERSON LIMITED

Toronto   Montreal   New York   St. Louis   San Francisco
Auckland   Bogotá   Düsseldorf   Johannesburg   London
Madrid   Mexico   New Delhi   Panama   Paris   São Paulo
Singapore   Sydney   Tokyo

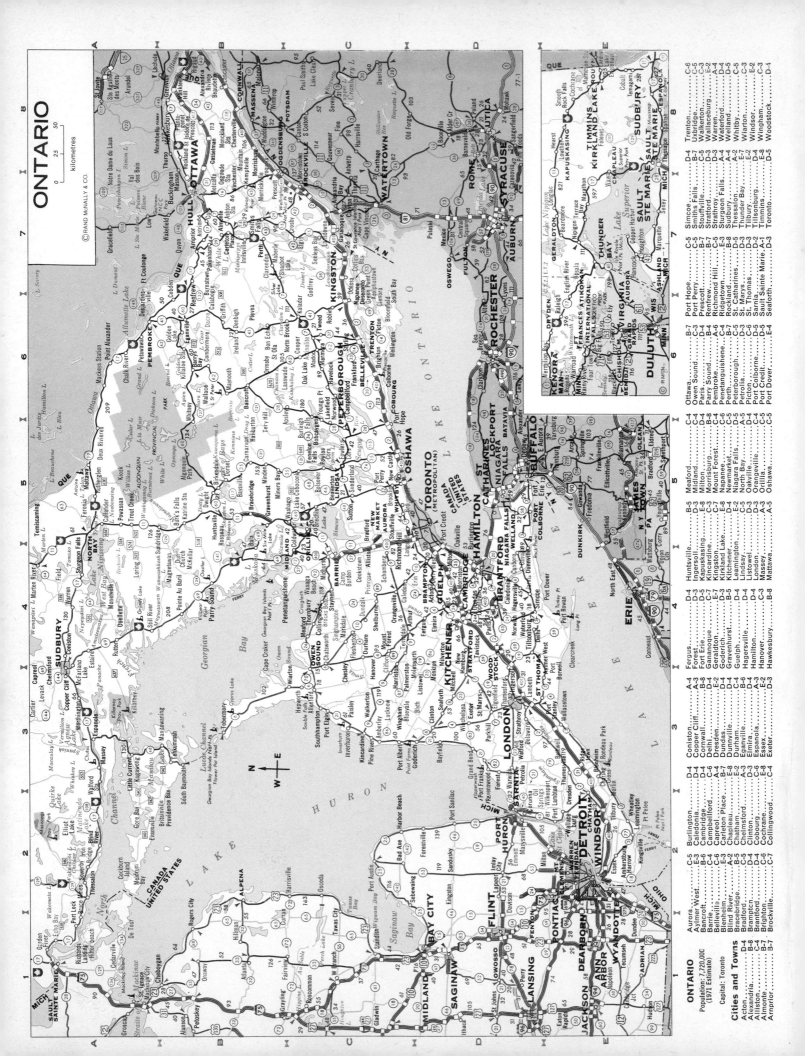

ONTARIO

kilometres

©RAND McNALLY & CO.

ONTARIO
Population: 7,720,000
(1971 Estimate)
Capital: Toronto

Cities and Towns

Aurora	D-4
Aylmer West	C-3
Bancroft	C-5
Barrie	D-4
Belleville	C-5
Blenheim	E-3
Blind River	A-2
Bracebridge	D-4
Bradford	D-4
Brampton	D-4
Brantford	D-4
Brighton	C-5
Brockville	B-7

Burlington	C-5
Caledonia	E-3
Cambridge	D-4
Campbellford	C-6
Capreol	C-4
Carleton Place	A-6
Chapleau	A-2
Chatham	E-8
Chelmsford	D-4
Clinton	D-3
Cobourg	C-5
Cochrane	C-6
Collingwood	C-7

Coniston	D-4
Copper Cliff	D-4
Cornwall	C-6
Delhi	C-6
Dresden	E-2
Dundas	B-7
Dunnville	C-4
Durham	C-4
Eganville	E-2
Elmira	D-3
Espanola	E-8
Essex	E-8
Exeter	C-4

Fergus	D-4
Forest	A-3
Gananoque	B-8
Geraldton	E-2
Goderich	C-7
Gravenhurst	C-4
Guelph	D-4
Hagersville	B-6
Hamilton	D-4
Hanover	C-3
Hawkesbury	B-8

Huntsville	D-3
Ingersoll	D-5
Kapuskasing	B-8
Kincardine	C-7
Kingston	C-6
Kirkland Lake	B-5
Kitchener	D-4
Leamington	E-2
Lindsay	D-5
Listowel	D-4
Lucknow	C-3
Massey	B-8
Mattawa	C-5

Meaford	B-5
Midland	D-3
Milton	D-5
Morrisburg	B-8
Mount Forest	C-7
Napanee	C-6
Niagara Falls	D-4
Niagara-on-the-Lake	D-5
North Bay	C-4
Oakville	D-5
Orangeville	D-3
Orillia	A-3
Oshawa	A-5

Ottawa	C-4
Owen Sound	C-4
Paris	B-8
Parry Sound	B-7
Pembroke	C-7
Penetanguishene	C-6
Perth	D-5
Peterborough	D-5
Pictou	D-5
Picton	C-6
Port Colborne	C-5
Port Credit	C-5
Port Dover	E-4

Port Hope	C-4
Port Perry	C-5
Prescott	D-4
Renfrew	C-5
Richmond Hill	E-5
Ridgetown	B-8
Rockland	C-3
St. Catharines	D-5
St. Marys	C-3
St. Thomas	A-2
Sarnia	E-2
Sault Sainte Marie	A-1
Seaforth	D-5

Simcoe	C-5
Smiths Falls	C-5
Stouffville	C-3
Stratford	D-3
Strathroy	A-4
Sturgeon Falls	C-4
Sudbury	D-5
Thessalon	A-2
Thunder Bay	E-2
Tilbury	E-2
Tillsonburg	E-8
Timmins	C-3
Toronto	D-4

Trenton	C-6
Uxbridge	C-5
Walkerton	C-3
Wallaceburg	E-2
Warren	A-4
Waterford	D-5
Welland	C-5
Whitby	A-2
Wiarton	C-3
Windsor	E-2
Wingham	E-8
Woodstock	D-4

Alexandria	E-2
Almonte	B-7
Arnprior	B-7

CONTENTS

ONTARIO

Nobody knows exactly what Ontario means. It is an Iroquoian name, and apparently refers to the waters of the great Lake Ontario or to the large rocks beside the lake — perhaps the Niagara Escarpment.

Whatever its meaning, Ontario was the name given to the lake by European visitors as early as 1641, and later to the county east of what is now Toronto. In 1867 it was applied to the whole of 'Canada West,' the second biggest of Confederation's founding provinces. It now stretches some 1600 km both north to south and east to west.

Today, Ontario is Canada's richest province and is also the most populated — though 90 percent of its 8.3 million population live in just one-sixth of the total area, far down in the south. The greatest density is in cities like Toronto, Hamilton, London, and Windsor in the south-west, and in the many smaller communities that surround them.

This is the area which has become Canada's industrial heart, not least because the geographic middle third of Canada's consumer market lies within 160 km of downtown Toronto. Development of the St. Lawrence Seaway in the 1950s made international ports of a dozen Ontario communities, and they have not been slow to profit.

Elsewhere in the province, there has been steady exploitation of rich resources in the north, particularly minerals and forests. Again, improved transport links have made all the difference. Progress in Eastern Ontario has not been so spectacular, but many of those who live there prefer the slower pace.

However, Ontario must not be judged by wealth alone. It offers great scope in the arts and in sport, whether for spectators or participants. Its scenery is varied and beautiful at all times of the year. And best of all, the harmony of its many cultures is a model for the rest of North America.

The trillium, also known as the wakerobin and white lily, was officially adopted as Ontario's floral emblem in 1937.

THE GLACIERS

Between 20 000 and 40 000 years ago, Ontario was smothered by a sheet of ice perhaps 2 km thick. The intruder was the Wisconsin, last in the series of glaciers which covered most of North America during the most recent 'Ice Age.'

The glaciers reshaped the terrain, their sheer weight scraping clean parts of the bedrock and gouging out depressions which much later filled with water. The process revealed the Canadian Shield, the geological core of North America. It is a fascinating jumble of rock formations between 600 million and three billion years old, perhaps the roots of ancient mountain systems.

Long before the glaciers arrived, these rock formations had been worn down by wind, water, and frost. Through thousands of years, layers of soil and vegetation had accumulated on their surface. When the glaciers came, rocks caught under the ice dug through the soil like ploughshares, and at many places the Shield remains starkly exposed to this day.

The glaciers also affected deposits of rock and organic matter laid down several million years ago — rock-hard sediment on the beds of ancient seas and river systems, which had washed the Shield both north and south. The sedi-

ments survive as the Hudson Bay lowlands and the lowlands of Southern Ontario.

In the south, the toughest sediment withstood erosion had now withstood the ice. But in melting some 10 000 years ago, the Wisconsin submerged the area in debris acquired on its long march — the rocks and soil scooped from the Shield. Much of it can still be traced in strange formations which occur throughout the province.

Southern Ontario contains several stretches of hilly moraine country, a legacy of the glaciers. These are near Orangeville in the Lake Simcoe district.

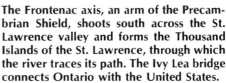

The Frontenac axis, an arm of the Precambrian Shield, shoots south across the St. Lawrence valley and forms the Thousand Islands of the St. Lawrence, through which the river traces its path. The Ivy Lea bridge connects Ontario with the United States.

The formations include 'moraines,' rolling hills of soil and gravel pushed up by the ice; 'eskers,' ridges formed as sediment by streams running within the melting glacier; and 'drumlins,' teardrop-shaped hillocks which resulted from the action of a later glacier on moraines left by an earlier one.

Soils in these southern areas, known as 'glacial till,' are much deeper and more fertile than the slightly acidic soils which have replaced them on the Shield. The richest deposits, those most favoured for agriculture and ideal for raising cash crops, are situated in the south-western peninsula and in the south-east.

The most extraordinary legacy of the glaciers is the world's largest body of fresh water, the Great Lakes. Lake Superior had been formed earlier through a fault in the Shield, but the other lakes of the chain were formed by erosion of the original sediments. Steady erosion over millions of years left depressions bounded by ridges of hard rock, like the Niagara Escarpment. The resulting basins were reshaped many times by advances and retreats of the glaciers and were eventually filled with fresh water as the Wisconsin melted.

All but one of the Great Lakes border Ontario, and the province has a freshwater shore of nearly 4000 km — as well as about 1000 km of saltwater

coastline along Hudson Bay.

Lake Superior is in a class by itself, being coldest and deepest of the five big lakes. Lakes Huron, Erie, and Ontario are sister formations which make a peninsula of south-western Ontario and wield great influence on its climate, as do Lakes Huron and Superior on Northern Ontario.

The ancient rocks of the Shield contain valuable mineral deposits. These include nickel, copper, zinc, iron ore, uranium, and the precious metals platinum, gold, and silver. In some sites six or more different metals have been found in one deposit.

The sediments of the lowland region hold rich resources of non-metals. South-western Ontario contains extensive saltbeds and also gypsum (both the residue of evaporated salt water), and limestone (deposited by an early sea). There are also deposits of natural gas and petroleum (the compacted remains of tiny plants and sea creatures).

Southern Ontario holds abundant supplies of sand and gravel essential to the construction industry. Gypsum and lignite (soft coal) have been found in the Hudson Bay lowlands, but so far it has not been feasible to exploit them.

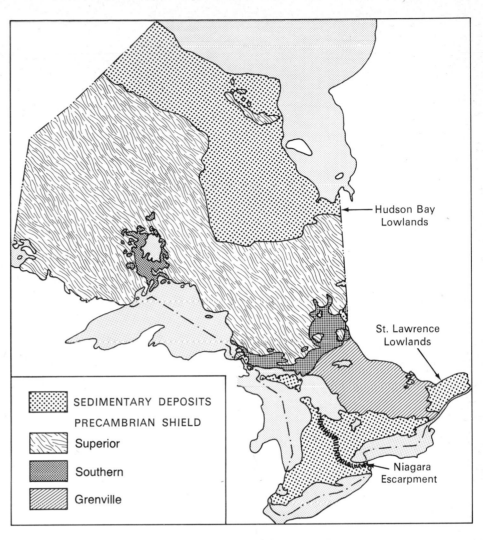

Hudson Bay Lowlands

St. Lawrence Lowlands

Niagara Escarpment

SEDIMENTARY DEPOSITS
PRECAMBRIAN SHIELD
Superior
Southern
Grenville

Near Toronto are the distinctive Scarborough Bluffs, cliffs of sandstone which are being slowly eroded by weather action and undermined by Lake Ontario, though current conservation efforts are minimizing this effect.

Geologists recognize separate 'provinces' in the Canadian Shield, classified by their formation. Most important of these provinces are Grenville, Southern, and Superior.

The Hudson Bay lowlands are characterized by static bodies of water which give rise to vast stretches of muskeg and quaking bogs of sphagnum moss, punctuated by scattered stands of black spruce.

THE WOODLANDS

Even excepting the Great Lakes, nearly one-fifth of Ontario is covered by water. Most of the rest is forested by deciduous hardwoods in the south and by immense areas of coniferous softwoods which blanket the north.

Ontario's forests can be considered as four zones, a neat succession running south to north. The smallest is the deciduous zone in the southern half of the south-western peninsula, really the northern tip of forests in the United States. Major species are sugar maple, beech, basswood, oak, and walnut. Only a fraction of the original deciduous forest remains because of the efforts of the pioneers, who cleared the land for agriculture.

The pioneers also denuded the southern fringe of the second zone — the 'mixed wood' forest stretching from Manitoba to the Ottawa valley, but this they did not penetrate deeply. In the mixed wood forest the major species include both hardwoods (sugar maple, white and yellow birch, red oak, white elm) and softwoods (white pine, hemlock, red pine, spruce, balsam fir). Less common are tamarack and white cedar (softwoods) and red maple, white oak, and basswood (hardwoods).

Beyond Lake Superior begins the great boreal forest of Ontario's northland — part of a forest band which extends around the globe. It consists chiefly of coniferous species, which to the unpracticed eye look the same. However there are big differences, particularly in cone shapes and branch formations. Major species in Ontario's boreal forest are black spruce, jack pine, and balsam fir, and less prolific are white spruce and some lesser species — poplar and white birch (both hardwoods) and tamarack. Acid in the needles dropped by the conifers means that there is different ground-level vegetation from that found in the mixed forest.

Towards its northern edge, the boreal forest is punctuated by barren stretches. Trees huddle in scattered groups to stand up to winter winds, and they grow much more slowly. Black spruce predominates in places, accompanied by the tamarack, which is paradoxically a deciduous conifer — it drops its leaves yet reproduces through cones.

The flat expanse of the Hudson Bay lowlands is badly drained and is characterized by unbroken stretches of muskeg bog. Muskeg is chiefly the result of constant plant growth which absorbs stagnant water from beneath. These lowlands, and the Shield as well, host a complex variety of bog types. Muskeg proper forms on shallow lakes and eventually becomes 'dry' bog, on which trees

Agawa canyon in the mixed-wood forest north of Sault Ste. Marie provides spectacular scenery for the run of the Algoma Central Railway.

can grow — the classic conversion of lake into dry land. But there are also 'raised' bogs, in which water is trapped and which raise water higher than the normal water table.

The contrasts between these vegetation zones are evidence of profound differences in soil and climate. By and large, soil on the Shield is shallow and acidic, apart from rare pockets of glacial debris. South of the Shield there is abundant fertile soil deposited by the glaciers, and in places this has been enriched by decaying vegetation full of nutrients.

Climatic division is on a different basis. In the south-western peninsula, winter temperatures are notably milder than elsewhere in Ontario, because of the Great Lakes and also because of latitude. South-eastern Ontario south of Lake Nipissing and the Laurentian Highlands have a 'continental' climate, with summers longer than winters.

Northern Ontario — five-sixths of the province — has winters longer than summers. Winter temperatures can plunge very low, and in the far north along Hudson Bay there are pockets of permafrost, where ground remains permanently frozen below certain depths. However, the short summer can be surprisingly warm.

The Quetico region north of Lake Superior is a maze of lakes and waterways interlacing the sprawling expanse of boreal forest. Lakes in the region are so numerous that most have not been named.

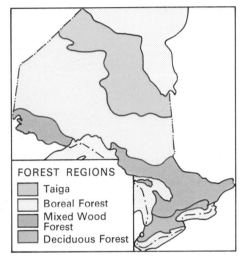

FOREST REGIONS
- Taiga
- Boreal Forest
- Mixed Wood Forest
- Deciduous Forest

Tree zones in Ontario follow a neat progression south to north.

The Rainy Lake area in Ontario's far western corner is rich in timber resources, and the waterways are used to transport pulpwood to nearby mills.

At winter's end, sugar maples of the hardwood forest are tapped for their sap. This is boiled to produce distinctive maple syrup, which is of major commercial significance.

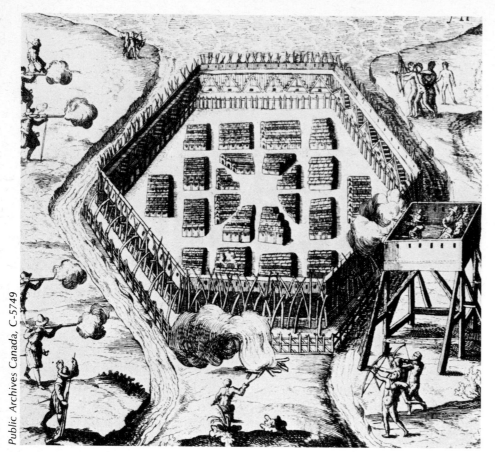

In 1615 the Hurons induced Samuel de Champlain and his French followers to join an expedition against the Onondagas near Lake Oneida, but the expedition was a failure. This engraving accompanied Champlain's account of the adventure (1632).

HURONS AND JESUITS

Early in the seventeenth century, the region between Georgian Bay and Lake Simcoe was the most populated in Canada. It was the home of the Huron Indians (a French slang term for their bristly hairstyles) and their neighbours the Petuns.

Both Hurons and Petuns were loose groupings of family-linked bands, living in scattered villages and subsisting by modest agriculture and fishing. They numbered about 25 000 — a match for their arch-rivals south of Lake Ontario, the Iroquois Confederacy of the Five Nations, and the less organized Algonquian peoples in the east.

Very soon after the founding of Quebec in 1608, Hurons travelled the river routes to the little colony to trade beaver pelts. There they encountered Samuel de Champlain, founder of New France, who proposed an exchange. He would take a Huron back to France, and his servant would spend a year with the Indians.

The servant was Etienne Brûlé, an enterprising teenager from Normandy. Brûlé soon adapted to the wilds, and in 1615 acted as interpreter when Cham- plain himself visited Georgian Bay with an armed escort. The Hurons were on the warpath against the Onondagas, the biggest of the Five Nations, and demanded that the French assist them. The party met the Iroquois near Lake Oneida but was beaten back — partly through incompetence, partly because promised reinforcements led by Brûlé did not arrive. Champlain was wounded twice and spent the winter recuperating in Huronia and exploring its villages. A close bond was established between the Hurons and the French.

In 1626 a small party of Jesuit missionaries led by Jean de Brébeuf penetrated Huronia. They had barely gained a foothold when they were obliged to withdraw. However, in 1634 Brébeuf and others were back. They built several small missions attached to villages, but were frustrated by serious outbreaks of smallpox, influenza, and dysentery.

In these years, too, the Hurons were plagued by the Five Nations, now equipped with firearms received from Dutch traders in the Hudson valley. After exhausting their own resources of beaver pelts, the Iroquois wanted those of the north. Raiding parties systematically broke up whole communities of Hurons and their neighbours.

The Jesuits reacted by constructing a

A 1660 engraving by Grégoire Huret shows the fate of Jesuit missionaries in Huronia. In the right foreground is Father Jean de Brébeuf, tortured by Iroquois, who pour boiling water over him in mockery of baptism, burn him with red-hot axeheads, and cut strips of flesh from his arms.

defensive headquarters in 1639 — Fort Ste. Marie, near present-day Midland. It was planned on a grand scale, equipped with church, school, farm, and hospital. From the fort, priests founded new missions in Huron villages, and had great success in making converts.

Things were quiet for nine years. Then in 1649 the peace ended. One of the Jesuits was celebrating mass at St. Joseph's mission, on the Coldwater river. There had been rumours that Iroquois were in the vicinity, and suddenly they were in the village. The priest was killed at his chapel door, and many Hurons were burned alive inside.

The next year another Iroquois war party looted the mission at St. Ignace, then went on to St. Louis, near what is now Victoria Harbour. They captured Brébeuf and another priest, took them back to St. Ignace, and tortured them with red-hot daggers and boiling water in mockery of baptism. Both were made to suffer for many hours before they were killed.

Though weakened by white men's diseases and fighting firearms with arrows, the main body of the Hurons rallied. They retook St. Louis, then met the fierce Iroquois at St. Ignace. After a long struggle they were defeated, and survivors not captured dispersed in panic. The great Huron nation was broken forever.

The missionaries left at Fort Ste. Marie burned it to the ground and

moved to a new site on Christian Island in Georgian Bay, where they believed they would be safe. Several thousand Hurons followed them, but that winter many died of hunger and many more of disease. A handful of Jesuits remained in villages of the Petuns.

In December 1649, an Iroquois war party killed a fourth Jesuit at St. Jean. The next day a fifth was murdered on his way to Christian Island — this time

A Huron long-house has been reconstructed at Ste. Marie-among-the-Hurons.

Jesuit headquarters in Huronia was the Fort Ste. Marie-among-the-Hurons near Midland, burned to the ground in 1640 when the missionaries abandoned it in the face of an Iroquois raiding party. The fort has been reconstructed from the evidence gained in intensive archaeological investigations.

by a Huron, who had known nothing but disaster since the arrival of the missionaries. In June 1650, all survivors of the Huron mission — 60 French and 300 Indians — left by canoe for Quebec.

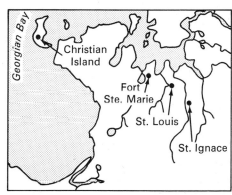

Before their extermination at the hands of the Iroquois, the Hurons and their neighbours occupied the region between Georgian Bay and Lake Simcoe.

UPPER CANADA

In 1749 the French built 'Fort Toronto' at the mouth of the Humber river, which was an important route to the interior. They aimed to prevent Indians from trading with the British, who had built a fortified post at Oswego, on the southern shore of Lake Ontario.

In 1758, during the Seven Years' War, a British force advanced on Fort Toronto. To prevent its capture, the French destroyed it. The next year the British burned down Fort Frontenac, an important French trading post on the site of present-day Kingston. It had been founded in 1673, chiefly to keep an eye on the Iroquois.

And so Southern Ontario returned to obscurity, while England ousted France from Quebec and the Americans rebelled against George III to claim their independence. As that revolution dragged towards its untidy conclusion, a trickle of Loyalist refugees from up-state New York and Pennsylvania settled in the Niagara Peninsula.

With the signing of the Treaty of Paris in 1763, the trickle became a steady stream. More Loyalists reached Niagara, and many others evacuated from the mouth of the Hudson river were resettled around present-day Cornwall. With them were British troops

Loyalists evacuated from the mouth of the Hudson river in New York were resettled in the area 'New Johnstown' (later Cornwall), Upper Canada, from 1783. James Peachey's painting of 1784 sets the scene.▼

Mohawk warriors of the Five Nations fought on the side of the British in the American War of Independence and were granted land in Upper Canada, on which they resettled. One tract was in the neighbourhood of Brantford, named after the Mohawk captain Joseph Brant. There the Mohawks erected a chapel under special patent of King George III, surviving today as Her Majesty's Royal Chapel of the Mohawks, the oldest Protestant place of worship in Ontario.

Encampment of the Loyalists at Johnstown, a New Settlement, on the Banks of the River S. Laurence in Canada, taken June 6 1784. taken from — marked in the Plan

Public Archives Canada, 29-1-18

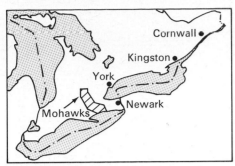

Upper Canada when John Graves Simcoe was lieutenant-governor, 1791–96.

disbanded after the war who preferred not to return home.

So many new arrivals posed problems for the British administration in Montreal. Surveyors were sent into 'Upper Canada' (as Ontario was then called) to mark out townships of several hundred hectares apiece, and to subdivide these townships into appropriate land lots. The land was granted to Loyalists and military according to their rank and resources.

Unoccupied land was in abundant supply, though it had to be cleared of dense forest. Every settler was issued an axe, hammer, saw, hoe, spade, nails, and a pair of door hinges. Each group of five families received a whipsaw for making planks and a gun for hunting. Seed was distributed, and in the early years food rations too.

Though living on a frontier, the Loyalists were more secure than most pioneers. They were immediately subject to organized government and were free of danger from Indian attacks. During the war, Mohawks of the Five Nations had fought for King George under their captain, Joseph Brant, and many of them had peacefully resettled north of Lake Erie.

Before long the settlers requested that they be governed separately from 'Lower Canada' (Quebec) and that they be granted their own elected assembly. In 1791 the British parliament passed the Constitutional Act and established similar forms of government for each colony in British North America. Upper Canada's first lieutenant-governor was John Graves Simcoe.

The same year Simcoe established his capital at Niagara-on-the-Lake, then named Newark. He chose an 'executive committee' of four, each selected as a

The site of York as sketched on birchbark by Elizabeth Simcoe.

man likely to impose a truly English stamp on the new province. Upper Canada's first assembly was duly elected and met in Newark in 1792.

Newark was too close to the American border to be safe as a capital, and so was Kingston, which had been refounded by disbanded military in 1783. It was the only other town in the province, and was prospering as a trade settlement. Simcoe wanted to establish a capital on the Thames river, on the site of what later became London, but he was overruled. The spot was considered too remote. Instead, he was obliged to use one of a series of possible naval bases that he had chosen, to preserve British supremacy on the Great Lakes. They included Kingston and Niagara, and a third on Georgian Bay, but the site selected was near the mouth of the Humber, the old site of Fort Toronto.

In spite of local objections, Simcoe named the new settlement 'York.' He arrived in 1793 with a naval and military detachment and laid out the town in ten blocks of 1.62 ha each. He also held a token meeting of his executive council in York in 1793, but from that time it met in Newark until permanent buildings in York were completed in 1797.

There had been stirrings to the south, and Simcoe was convinced that Americans might attempt an invasion. Accordingly he took steps to link his potential naval bases by military roads. 'Yonge Street' was to run north to Georgian Bay, and 'Dundas Street' from Detroit through York to Kingston.

John Graves Simcoe   Elizabeth Simcoe

Upper Canada's beginnings were dominated by John Graves Simcoe, first lieutenant-governor (1791–96), and his wife Elizabeth, who kept a careful diary and drew prolific sketches. One was of the embryonic Kingston, established by disbanded military and soon the major settlement of Upper Canada.

The towns of Fort William and Port Arthur were combined to form the city of Thunder Bay. A replica of old Fort William has been constructed not far from Thunder Bay but not on its original site.

THE NOR'WESTERS

In spite of colonization, the chief route to Canada's west remained as it had been in Champlain's day. Voyageurs and Indians paddled up the Ottawa and Mattawa rivers, across Lake Nipissing, and down the French river to Georgian Bay.

From there, canoes hugged the northern shoreline of Lakes Huron and Superior, until they reached the Grand Portage at the mouth of the Pigeon river. Then the travellers headed for the Great Plains, the Rocky Mountains, and perhaps the Western Sea. In a century, this vast area had been opened for the fur trade.

Originally the fur trade had been shared by two balanced groups — the French of Montreal, who concentrated on the south, and the English of Hudson Bay, who had been granted possession of all 'Rupert's Land' by a charter of Charles II. But in the wake of England's

victory at Quebec, aggressive Scots traders entered the arena.

The Scotsmen had scant respect for Rupert's Land and went wherever they wanted — particularly in the north-west, which had the best fur. They were prepared to trade with Indians on the spot, in their own encampments. The English realized what was happening only when the number of Indians visiting their posts sharply declined.

Belatedly, the English established themselves in the interior. But by now the Scots were prospering. Those longest established could remain in Montreal, while junior wintering partners worked in the field. In the 1770s several partnerships joined forces, and by 1784 they had consolidated as the North West Company.

The new partners took steps to improve efficiency. Already hundreds of men worked for them directly — French

voyageurs, Métis, and Indians — and their system revolved around Grand Portage. To and from that point, trusted voyageurs ferried trade goods and brought back beaver pelts delivered from the interior each summer.

In 1797 the partners constructed a lock system at the rapids of Sault Ste. Marie, the gateway to Lake Superior. This allowed them to use substantially larger craft on the main delivery run. Besides this, they voted money to improve the portage route from York to Lake Huron, and for the use of schooners on Lake Ontario.

In 1800 the Americans claimed that Grand Portage was in their territory and set up a customs post. The partners bypassed it by establishing new headquarters farther north — Fort William on Thunder Bay, named after William McGillivray, who was chief director of the company. It was completed in stages

William McGillivray

Oil painting attributed to Martin Shee.

Lord Selkirk

Prime protagonists in the fate of the North West Company were both Scottish-born. William McGillivray was chief director of the company, the man after whom Fort William on Thunder Bay was named. Lord Selkirk was a philanthropist aiming to re-establish poor Highland colonists in what is now Manitoba.

between 1801 and 1805.

At this time the Hudson's Bay Company was in serious trouble. Though unable to conquer England, Napoleon had decreed an embargo on trade with England by any European nation, and the company's fur market dried up. However its loss was apparently the Nor'Westers' gain, for resourcefully they sold more furs than ever.

The Nor'Westers held an annual convention at Fort William. Each summer some of the partners from Montreal made their way to the fort with great convoys of voyageur canoes. There they met the wintering partners and the *coureurs de bois* from the interior — the men of the front line who visited every corner of the north-west.

Voyageurs from French Canada travelled throughout North America in search of furs. This oil painting, *Voyageurs at Dawn*, is by Mrs. F. A. Hopkins (1871).

So things continued for years, until in 1811 there was a setback. The Hudson's Bay Company had granted a vast tract of land to the Scottish philanthropist Lord Selkirk, who planned to resettle displaced Highlanders. The area concerned directly blocked the Nor'-Westers' routes to the interior — which was no doubt what their rivals intended.

The Nor'Westers fought the new settlement with every means at their disposal. Then in 1816, following a pitched battle at Red River, Lord Selkirk himself arrived at Fort William with a detachment of armed men. It was the time of the annual convention, there were many thousands in residence, and nearly all the directors were present. Selkirk demanded — and received — the surrender of William McGillivray. He also arrested the other directors and marooned the trappers and voyageurs on the other side of the river. He took possession of the fort as 'the last of any in the British dominions, as an asylum for banditti and murderers, and the receptacle for their plunder.'

The courts later condemned Selkirk's actions, but he had defeated the Nor'Westers. With Napoleon a prisoner, the Hudson's Bay Company was again competitive, and under new direction it quickly took advantage of its shorter transport route to the interior. Urged by the British government, the rivals amalgamated in 1821.

Fort William, field headquarters of the North West Company, was built in stages between 1801 and 1805 but lost influence following the amalgamation of the North West Company and the Hudson's Bay Company in 1821. This is a watercolour of the fort by William H. E. Napier (1857).

The Battle of Queenston Heights, as pictured in a contemporary aquatint by James Dennis. This was the action in which Sir Isaac Brock was killed while trying to drive American invaders from high ground. The Americans were later repelled and driven back across the river.

The Battle of the Thames in Moraviantown, 1813. Here Tecumseh was killed, and the American success gave invaders a strong foothold in south-western Ontario. (An anonymous lithograph.) ▼

Tecumseh

Sir Isaac Brock

Twin heroes of the War of 1812, at least in its early stages, were the British commander Isaac Brock and the Indian leader Tecumseh. Together they met early threats of invasion by the United States and restored Upper Canada's confidence in itself. But both men were killed — Brock at Queenston Heights in 1812, and Tecumseh at Moraviantown in 1813.

Laura Secord was a Loyalist living in Queenston. In June 1813 she learned of plans for a surprise attack on Beaver Dam from American troops billeted in her house. She walked nearly 36 km through American lines to bring word to Lieutenant James

FitzGibbon, who was in charge of Beaver Dam. He had already heard of the planned attack through Indians, but Laura Secord's effort has secured her continuing gratitude in Canada. Her house in Queenston has been preserved.

WAR IN 1812

The conflict which Simcoe had anticipated flared up in 1812. Taking advantage of Britain's preoccupation with Napoleon, the United States declared war. The reasons stated chiefly concerned British naval harassment of American merchant shipping. However, most of the American ships affected were from New England and New York, and these states opposed retaliation. 'War Hawks' in the American congress were from the south and the west. They saw a chance to drive the British out of Canada, and also to destroy Indian power in the Great Lakes region.

The Americans selected Upper Canada as their prime target. Thousands of Americans had settled there, and it was assumed that they would support their compatriots. These settlers were not Loyalists, but ordinary Americans who had taken advantage of the free land available.

General Isaac Brock, who had recently been appointed provisional lieutenant-governor, was commanding the military in Upper Canada. He was short of regular troops and believed his best hope of survival lay in persuading the Indians to side with him. When war broke out, he quickly ordered the capture of an American fort south of Sault Ste. Marie.

The success impressed the Indians, and particularly the great Shawnee chief, Tecumseh, who had grudges to settle with the Americans. Together he and Brock prepared a daring raid on Detroit, where they captured 2500 men without a shot fired. It showed doubters in Upper Canada that their cause was not hopeless.

From Detroit Brock moved to the Niagara Peninsula, where a second American army was preparing to invade Canadian soil. Driven from Queenston Heights, Brock rallied some of his men to charge the position, but he was killed in the attempt. The British later forced the Americans to withdraw, but the loss of Brock had crippled their initiative.

Instead, the war settled down to long periods of stalemate. There was an uneasy balance of power at both ends of Lake Erie, though this was disrupted when the Americans built a squadron of ships on the lake and seized naval initiative. But on Lake Ontario the British were building ships in Kingston and held the Americans in check.

The peace on Lake Ontario was broken, however, in April 1813. A strong American force crossed by schooner and raided York. After fierce fighting most of the British garrison withdrew, but before leaving they mined their magazine. It exploded and killed scores of the invaders as well as many civilians.

Enraged, the Americans looted the settlement, then set fire to Simcoe's government buildings. But rather than hold the base, they returned across the lake, taking with them quantities of plunder. This included Upper Canada's ceremonial mace. In 1814 the British retaliated by burning government buildings in Washington.

As the war progressed it became more bitter. Canadian militia from Upper Canada fought fiercely alongside the British regulars, particularly when raiding Americans burned and looted their property. Upper Canada had been settled barely three decades before, but the war compacted the scattered families and made them a nation.

The Americans succeeded in only one of their objectives. They had pledged themselves to break Indian power in the lakes, and in October 1813 they killed Tecumseh at Moraviantown on the Thames river. He alone wielded influence enough to rally his people to fight the 'Long Knives,' and with his passing their resistance died.

In 1814 the British were freed from the menace of Napoleon and could turn their full attention to the American problem. With the pressures of the war, the United States treasury was running dangerously low. Even the Hawks were inclined to make peace, and it was signed on Christmas Eve at Ghent in Belgium.

THE REFORMERS

One result of the war was that the British government decided to encourage immigration to the Canadas. It hoped to build a large population with British sympathies. Free land was offered to Scots, English, and Irish, most of it in Upper Canada.

At this time there was great economic distress in the British Isles. The industrial revolution was in progress, and in many cases machines had replaced skilled workers. At the same time the birthrate soared. Between 1820 and 1850, more than one and a half million people sailed the Atlantic to the Canadas in hopes of a better life.

In a short period the face of Upper Canada changed beyond recognition. A patchwork of homesteads and villages had opened up the countryside. Commercial centres like York and Kingston were thriving. Other communities were growing — Cornwall, Cobourg, Belleville, Peterborough, London, Niagara, Waterloo, Chatham, and Simcoe.

With their enterprise, some of the immigrants brought new political attitudes. Fresh from long campaigns promoting electoral reform in Britain, they found the new colonies backward. Upper Canada's legislative assembly was elected, but real power lay with the lieutenant-governor and his executive council. This was a body appointed by the lieutenant-governor, and it was so cliquish that it was nicknamed the Family Compact. Would-be reformers argued that it should be elected like the assembly. Its most violent critic was William Lyon Mackenzie, a newspaper editor who had arrived from Scotland in 1820. Mackenzie was elected to the assembly in 1828, but was expelled for libel in 1831.

Mackenzie continued his campaign on constitutional lines but made little headway. In frustration he turned to force of arms, and during 1837 drilled several hundred volunteers. One night in December they marched on Toronto, but they were repelled by twenty-seven militiamen. A few days later, loyal troops marched up Yonge Street and routed the rebels near Montgomery's tavern.

Mackenzie escaped to the United States. Within a week he was established at Navy Island, upstream of Niagara Falls, and launched a 'provisional government of the State of Upper Canada.' He was supplied by American sympathizers until Canadians seized and burned their ship the *Caroline.*

In 1838 bands of Americans in 'Hunters' Lodges' tried to liberate Canada and were repelled in a series of skirmishes in Eastern Ontario. Lord Durham, sent to the Canadas as governor-general to restore order, urged the British government to unite the Canadas. He advocated 'responsible government,' in which the executive council would be responsible to the legislature.

The British government proclaimed an 'Act of Union' in 1841, by which the two Canadas were combined under one governor and council and one elected assembly. But 'Canada East' and 'Canada West' were granted equal

Mackenzie's supporters rallied at Montgomery's tavern in Toronto, which stood on Yonge Street near its present junction with Eglinton Avenue. There a Colonel Moodie of the local militia shot at them when attempting to ride through a rebel roadblock and was killed when his fire was returned.

DEATH OF COL. MOODIE.

View of the Battle of Windmill Point, below Prescott, Upper Canada, (from the Ogdensburg side of the St. Lawrence) November 13, 1838.

As the aftermath of Upper Canada's rebellion, in 1838 Americans belonging to various frontier 'Hunters' Lodges' attempted to liberate Canada, in sympathy with reformers who had fled Upper Canada. But they were easily driven off. This was a skirmish around a windmill at Prescott, on the St. Lawrence river opposite Ogdensburg, New York.

Public Archives Canada, C-4788

Following the Battle of Montgomery's tavern, Mackenzie and his followers fled to the United States and soon set up a provisional government on Navy Island, in the Niagara river. The *Caroline*, the American ship which supplied them, was boarded by loyal Canadians in December 1837 and set on fire, as represented in this aquatint by G. Tattersall.

numbers of seats in the assembly, which suggested federation rather than union; and the assembly was often frustrated when the Council blocked proposed legislation.

Besides, there was little evidence of responsible government. Executive council members were selected from the assembly, but were appointed by the governors concerned as before. Then in 1847 a new governor arrived — Lord Elgin, the son-in-law of Lord Durham. He was prepared to implement Durham's suggestions.

An election early in 1848 brought reformers to power in both provinces. Elgin sanctioned a joint ministry led by Robert Baldwin of Canada West, who was long prominent in the reform movement, and Louis LaFontaine of Canada East. In three years it made swift progress towards reorganizing municipal government and improving the judicial system.

In 1849 the Canadas' parliament moved to Toronto following riots in Montreal, and for the next decade it periodically migrated between Toronto and Quebec City. Meanwhile, it was agreed to establish a permanent capital at Bytown, renamed Ottawa. Bytown's advantage was that it was not vulnerable to attack from the United States.

Fair, proportional representation in parliament would have favoured Canada West, since its population was now bigger, so the idea was strongly opposed by reformers in Canada East. The result was a succession of weak governments, the more worrying since in the United States covetous eyes were turned on British North America's unoccupied west.

Throughout this turmoil emerged the steadying influence of John A. Macdonald, who had arrived as a child immigrant in the same year as Mackenzie and who had grown up in Kingston. In partnership with George-Etienne Cartier of Canada East, Macdonald sealed the coalition of Moderates and Conservatives which promoted the union of British North America.

Baldwin   **W. L. Mackenzie**

William Lyon Mackenzie was the moving spirit of the reform movement in its early years — first as a journalist, then as a member of Upper Canada's legislative assembly and first mayor of Toronto, and ultimately as a revolutionary. Among his supporters was Robert Baldwin, who in 1841 played a major role in the joint ministry which saw the introduction of responsible government.

17

INDUSTRIAL GROWTH

The great trees of Upper Canada's forests were valuable to early settlers as construction materials and as fuel. Trees cleared from the land were also burned, and the residue was processed as potash and exported to Europe to make soap and fertilizer.

In 1851 there were 277 asheries in Upper Canada, but by that time another timber industry had been developed. The great white pines of Upper Canada found ready markets both in Europe and the United States. Rafts of timber were floated down the rivers to ports on the St. Lawrence or across the Great Lakes to the United States.

At first all timber was 'squared' for use in shipbuilding. Later, water-powered sawmills were introduced to satisfy the needs of settlers wanting to improve on the crude log cabins built in the early days. In 1840 there were 1400 sawmills in the province. Most of them were modest operations, but some were much larger, catering to the export trade.

From an early stage, the government of Upper Canada had supported construction of these mills by making generous loans to those prepared to erect and operate them. In the same way a number of grain-mills (400 in 1840) and a few wool-mills were established, which were also water-powered in most cases. They, too, encouraged more farmers to settle.

Winter wheat was a favourite crop with the new settlers, particularly when an export market to Britain developed in 1843. The British government allowed Canadian wheat and flour to enter duty free, and in a few years milling capacity doubled. But in 1849 the British dropped tariff protection, and the advantage was lost.

The growth of trade and commerce was supported by the expansion of transport networks. The forty-lock Welland Canal was completed in the 1830s to bypass Niagara Falls. It provided a water route between Lakes Erie and Ontario. Already a series of short canals and lock systems helped ships to navigate the upper St. Lawrence.

The 1850s were the great age of railway building. The first line opened in Upper Canada was the Great West

Railway between Niagara and Windsor via Hamilton, soon connected with Toronto. But it was overshadowed by the Grand Trunk from Montreal, which reached Toronto in 1856 and continued to Detroit by its own route.

The first significant manufacturing industry arose from the wheat harvest. Several small firms began producing mechanical reapers and other tools, particularly the Massey company established in Newcastle and the Harris companies of Beamsville and Brant County. Both utilized American railway systems to market their products in the west.

The Massey Company of Toronto, forerunner of today's Massey-Ferguson, achieved international fame for its lightweight Toronto binder.

The little Canadian companies developed machines far superior in design and performance to their American counterparts, and in the 1870s they began exporting them worldwide. In agricultural trials they were triumphant everywhere, but the Canadian companies found rivalry so wasteful that they joined forces in 1891 and promptly absorbed their leading local competitors too.

With the opening of Western Canada, many Ontario wheat farmers moved to the Prairies. Those who remained concentrated on mixed farming in the tradition of the Loyalists, with a balanced emphasis on crops and livestock. Many bred horses for western agriculture and the forest industries, and even for American streetcars.

Elsewhere in the Canadas, there was steady development of other primary industries. There was commercial freshwater fishing on the Great Lakes, with markets in the United States. In the north many Indians and others still lived by trapping. There was spasmodic mining of copper and silver in the north-west, and of copper and iron ore in the east.

Canada's first oil field was developed in the south-west. In 1859 James Miller Williams sank Canada's first commercial well at Oil Springs, in 'gum beds' previously used to make asphalt. Drilling began there in 1861-62.

In 1861 the Petrolia field was discovered nearby.

At that time oil was important not as petroleum but as the source of kerosene. Prospectors combed the district, scores of wells were drilled, and rickety 'refineries' went into production. Communities affected by the boom included London, which thrived at its centre, and Goderich, where test drilling revealed vast saltbeds.

Buildings transported from communities that were flooded to make the St. Lawrence Seaway have been assembled at Upper Canada Village near Morrisburg, between Kingston and Cornwall. The village is the most extensive of Ontario's various re-created communities and gives a fine idea of nineteenth century life in the province.

North America's first commercial oilwells were developed in the region of Petrolia, Southern Ontario, in 1857.

Alexander Graham Bell first spelled out his notion of a telephone during a conversation with his father, who lived in this house in Brantford, in 1874. In 1876 Bell sent the first long-distance call on the telegraph wire from Brantford to Paris, Ontario.

THE ECONOMY

In 1867 the two Canadas, New Brunswick, and Nova Scotia joined forces in Confederation, with John A. Macdonald stead, these activities are concentrated in the south.

Manufacturing is strong, and Ontario accounts for more than 50 per cent of Canada's total output of finished goods.

Besides, a high proportion is exported to the United States and other countries. It amounts to nearly 40 per cent of Canada's total exports of fabricated goods.

Of these manufactured products, the

The Precambrian Shield of Ontario's northland provides a rich store of minerals. This is an open-pit mining operation at Mattabi, north of Lake Superior, producing copper, zinc, and other metals.

Ontario's agriculture is rich and diverse. This is a vineyard in the Niagara region, the home of Ontario wine production. ▼

of Kingston as their first prime minister. Canada East became Quebec and Canada West became the Province of Ontario, with Toronto as its capital.

However, one major factor in Ontario is that population and employment opportunities are unevenly distributed. Ninety per cent of the population lives in Southern Ontario — the area south of the Mattawa and French rivers, the old portage route. Geographically, that leaves Northern Ontario's size as five-sixths of the whole of the province.

It is in Northern Ontario that much of the primary industry is concentrated. Primary industry includes most of the mining and logging, as well as metal recovery and pulp and paper operations, which properly belong in the secondary sector. But agriculture is sparse, and there is limited potential for manufacturing and construction. In-

most important single category is transportation equipment, and particularly motor vehicles and automotive parts. The food and beverage sector is the second biggest category, and then primary metals and metal fabricating, electrical products, chemicals and chemical products, machinery, and pulp and paper.

The construction industry, the second largest element in the goods-producing sector, thrives in response to general prosperity. It includes not only residential and industrial construction, but also transportation projects, such as the building of roads and airports, and projects concerned with electrical power.

cial management, and in some views even the public service. In Ontario the tertiary sector has grown steadily in proportion to the other two.

As regards the work force, the service sector accounts for about 65 per cent of all jobs. Manufacturing and construction account for a further 30 per cent, and the primary industries for the tiny remainder. Unemployment generally runs below the national average.

Confederation was economic as well as political. Canadian manufacturers had prospered during the American Civil War, which had allowed them to develop home markets without American competition. Political union with an external tariff protected local enterprise and encouraged development of strong transport links in both the east and the west.

Major petrochemical complexes have been developed in Sarnia on Lake Huron, fed chiefly by crude oil from Canada's western provinces.

In the primary sector, Ontario produces about 20 per cent of Canada's total output of minerals, and over 30 per cent if fossil fuels are excluded. Metals are especially important, particularly nickel, copper, zinc, and iron ore. Besides these minerals, the province produces nearly 40 per cent of Canada's structural materials, such as gravel and cement.

In agriculture, Ontario's cash receipts amount to about 25 per cent of Canada's total, making it the largest agricultural producer. The province is characterized by mixed farming, but a wide range of specialty crops is also produced. Corn and tobacco are among the most lucrative.

Tertiary industry involves the many services necessary to conduct the primary and secondary sectors. These include transport, energy production, retail trade, repairs, catering, banking, finan-

Initial industrial progress in Ontario was slow, for Quebec and particularly Montreal provided most consumer goods. But gradually the west was settled, and this was a market from which Ontario could profit. As immigrants reached Ontario — many to continue west — a number of them, at least, turned to trade and commerce.

And that is the pattern that has persisted to the present. Ontario has a greater population than any other province — 8.3 million of Canada's 23 million in 1976. The province contributes some 40 per cent of Canada's gross national product, and its residents have consistently earned more than the national average.

Of course, Ontario has many natural advantages. They include its geographic position, the prime agricultural land, and the dense forest which first attracted the pioneers. In addition it has rich mineral resources and considerable water power from streams and rivers. These features were especially significant in encouraging private enterprise.

The telecommunications industry has boomed in recent decades, and much of Ontario's manufacturing sector is directly concerned with it. This is an electrical wiring plant in Brampton, near Toronto.

AGRICULTURE

Ontario's agricultural base is broader than that of any other province. More than one hundred different commodities are produced, ranging from widespread grain and livestock to specialty crops like tobacco, grapes, and vegetables.

All but a fraction of agricultural activity is confined to Southern Ontario, and in particular to the south-west peninsula and the triangle at the junction of the St. Lawrence and Ottawa valleys. These are the areas richest in glacial till. Besides, the peninsula's southern half has mild winters due to Lakes Erie and Ontario.

This is the region which provides so much diversity. Grapes and tender fruits thrive in the Niagara Peninsula, and several counties grow tobacco and soybeans. The two counties farthest west raise specialty crops unique to Canada because of the area's special climate. But ironically, this whole region attracts industrial development and urban sprawl more than any other.

Not that the land involved is extensive, in comparison to the arable land available elsewhere in the province, but it alone can produce certain fruits and vegetables which in times of shortage could prove invaluable. That would be impossible if it was built over. Some people say that the region's soil is a national resource and should be safeguarded.

The crisis in the south-west is unfortunate, because otherwise Ontario has immense tracts of arable land. Most of it is of much poorer grade and with far worse climate, but less than half has been developed. Much former agricultural land is lying idle because farmers can make no profit from it.

Farmers work to produce higher returns from their efforts, like other sectors of the community. As production costs rise, it has become more obvious that farming is a business. For example, groups of farmers band together as 'co-operatives' to buy feed, fertilizer, and other supplies at lower prices than would otherwise be possible.

The need for consistent sales levels for each commodity has encouraged the rise of marketing boards. These are elected by the producers concerned and are recognized by the provincial gov-

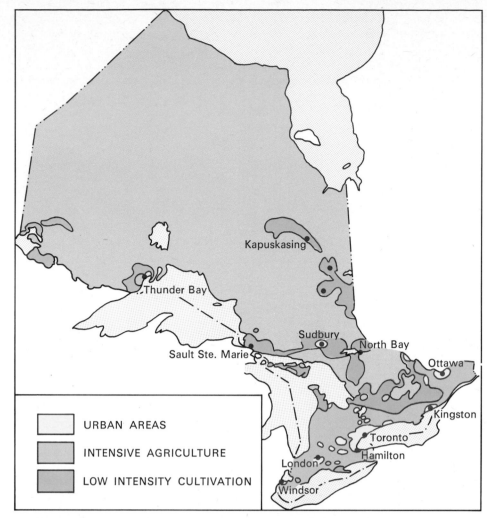

URBAN AREAS

INTENSIVE AGRICULTURE

LOW INTENSITY CULTIVATION

Ontario is endowed with fertile soil in the south-west and in the St. Lawrence lowlands. The south-west has mild winters because of the moderating influence of the Great Lakes.

Recent years have seen steady expansion of South Ontario's cornlands, as a result of the introduction of a number of robust hybrid varieties.

The pride of south-western Ontario is the fruitlands of the Niagara Peninsula, at their best in the blossom-time of early spring.

ernment as the producers' representatives. Each has its own scheme, but most aim to regulate sales by setting prices or imposing quotas, or by negotiating with buyers and processors on the producers' behalf.

More than twenty such boards operate in Ontario. Among those with high profiles are the province's milk board and pork producers' board, and the flue-cured tobacco growers' board, which has one eye on the export market. The Ontario boards concerned with egg and poultry production have worked with equivalent boards in other provinces to establish a national scheme.

Compared with the situation in earlier decades, Ontario's farms today are fewer, larger, more mechanized, and more productive. This is partly the result of a steady population drift from the land into industry and commerce (though there are indications that this has stopped), and partly because labour is so expensive that farmers have been forced to invest a considerable amount of capital in machinery.

At the same time there has been a quickening trend towards specialization. Some livestock operations seem more like factories than farms, and today's young farmer in Ontario is quite possibly a university graduate. He is supported by a range of research and advisory services provided by both provincial and federal authorities.

There has been a steady increase in part-time farmers who derive much of their income from an outside job. In Northern Ontario many loggers, miners, and others have bought farms as lucrative sidelines. In the south, the part-time farm provides many with the chance to 'get back to the land.'

Activity on the farm slows down appreciably during the winter months, though livestock needs as much care as in other seasons.

Vegetable growers are concentrated near major population centres. This is a cabbage harvest, destined for the fresh vegetable markets of Toronto and surrounding communities.

MILK AND LIVESTOCK

Two-thirds of Ontario's farm income is from livestock and livestock products, such as milk and eggs. This production makes up more than a third of Canada's total output. Besides, a high proportion of crop production is utilized as livestock feed.

The majority of livestock farms in Ontario stock herds of breeding cattle, either beef or dairy (though with dairy cattle, breeding is secondary to milk production). The total herd of breeding cows has remained constant for many years, but there has been a major change in its composition. The dairy herd has steadily decreased, while the beef cow-calf herd has doubled since 1965.

Most beef cow-calf operations are concentrated in less fertile agricultural areas, not least in Northern Ontario and Manitoulin (the world's largest freshwater island, located in Georgian Bay). Most of these farms grow their own hay and perhaps some corn and grain, as

well as produce livestock. These they sell young or raise to maturity, when they are ready for slaughter.

Depending on the state of the market, the calves sold may be slaughtered as veal or may be reared in specialist feedlots. These are located in the south-western corn belt. Cattle are encouraged to put on weight as swiftly and economically as possible, so that they will be ready for the stock sales. However, Ontario feedlots buy most of their replacement stock from Alberta and Saskatchewan.

These days 75 per cent of the beef cattle in Ontario are Herefords, but crossbreeds are increasingly popular. The breeder crosses lines long-established in Canada, like the Aberdeen Angus and Shorthorn, with hefty, faster-growing newcomers, like the Charolais and Simmental. Most breeders have their own bulls.

The typical Ontario dairy herd consists of forty cows. Again the farmer normally grows most of their feed — probably grass and legumes as summer

pasture, and corn as silage for winter, when the cows are penned in a barn. In Eastern Ontario dairy production outweighs other forms of agriculture, though there are more dairy cattle in the southwest, where cash crops and beef production are more lucrative.

The mainstay of the milking herd is the Holstein, followed at a great distance by Ayrshires, Jerseys, and Guernseys. The herd produces as much milk as in the past, but improved breeding and feeding means that fewer cows can produce a higher yield. Surplus calves (usually male) are slaughtered as veal or perhaps are reared as beef if the market justifies it.

Because of the corn crop, Ontario is Canada's leading producer of swine. Some farmers keep sows to farrow 'weanlings,' which they sell; some fatten these weanlings for market; but most

Beef cattle — in this case Herefords — are mature and ready for sale in feedlots — large pens in which they are encouraged to put on weight as quickly as possible.

Turkey farming accounts for a significant proportion of Ontario's poultry production, with young turkeys reared in long barns until ready for slaughter. Canadians eat more poultry — especially at Thanksgiving and Christmas — than any other nation.

Swine are fattened for market in clean, well-lit barns, where they are fed a controlled diet of pellets.

specialists run farrow-to-finish operations. Normally swine are housed in clean, warm, well-lit barns and are fed a controlled diet of pellets.

Two swine breeds are traditional in Ontario — the Landrace and the Yorkshire, which are known as 'whites.' Many breeders cross white sows with meatier breeds like the Duroc and Hampshire from the United States. The whites contribute litter size, while the American boars contribute growth rate.

Once Ontario had an impressive sheep population, but it has steadily declined because of low returns on lamb and mutton (let alone wool). On the other hand, the demand for lamb steadily increases among certain immigrant groups, and prices may recover. Important breeds are the Suffolk, Hampshire, Dorset, Leicester, and North Country Cheviot.

Poultry and egg production is probably the most sophisticated sector in Canadian agriculture, and it is also the most specialized. Most farms concentrate on eggs or on broiler chickens, but some produce fertilized eggs for broiler producers or day-old chicks for egg farmers. In Ontario many specialize in turkeys.

The battery farming techniques pioneered by egg producers are mirrored in dairy and swine operations — at least in feeding techniques. Beef feedlots rely on the principles pioneered by mass broiler and turkey producers, who aim to raise fowl for slaughter quickly and economically in terms of the feed they consume.

Holsteins are the mainstay of Ontario's dairy industry. Here a small herd is driven back to the farm, ready for milking.

CASH CROPS

A big share of Ontario's crop production is fed to livestock on the farm, so it does not earn direct cash income. But the province is responsible for all but a fraction of Canada's corn and tobacco crop, 70 per cent of its vegetables, and all of its soybeans.

Corn was grown by the Indians of Huronia long before the arrival of white men, but until 1960 commercial production was limited to a few counties in the mild south-west. Since then a number of robust hybrid varieties have been introduced, and the hectarage under corn doubled in the 1960s and has increased as crops are grown farther east.

A corn crop is attractive because it is relatively easy to grow, yet yields greater value per hectare than any other cereal. However, this advantage is offset by the need for greater outlay on fertilizer, herbicides, and insecticides. On the other hand, a corn crop has good years and bad years but it never fails entirely.

Early in May the farmer plants hybrid seed appropriate to local soil and climate, and a few weeks later sprays his fields with herbicides and insecticides. He can then shut the gate on his field until harvest time in mid-October, which normally continues well into November or for as long as weather permits.

All aspects of corn production are mechanized (as happens with nearly all cash crops). But in the case of corn, the seed can be sown without the soil being tilled first. The Ontario crop is almost entirely 'dent' corn, used chiefly as animal feed (whether on the home farm, or on other farms in or outside Ontario). The corn is harvested either as grain or the whole plant is finely chopped to be stored for winter.

In recent years many farmers of the south-west have grown winter wheat, which produces less yield than corn per hectare but is less costly to grow. In this case the farmer ploughs his fields in August and sows them six weeks later. Ideally the wheat grows 10 to 15 cm before the winter freeze — enough to support winter snow without being exposed.

The crop is dormant throughout the winter but should stay green, then it

A wide variety of vegetables are grown in south-western Ontario. Among the most distinctive is the pumpkin.

Most of Ontario's corn crop, which is harvested by combines, is used as animal feed. It is harvested either as grain or as the whole plant finely chopped to be stored for winter. ▼

Durham County is the centre of Ontario's tobacco lands, distinguished by sandy soil with good drainage. Close to the crop are the curing kilns and drying barns, in which harvested leaves are prepared for market.

Farmers say that hay is the easiest crop to grow although probably the most difficult to harvest. But the task has been made easier through the introduction of self-propelled swather-crushers, which lay the hay in swaths ready for drying.

Hay, on the other hand, is very important. It is the easiest crop to grow but it is the most difficult to harvest. The traditional method is to mow it, then rake it to help it dry, then bale it. Some farmers use self-propelled swather-crushers, which lay the hay in swaths. Later a forage harvester chops it ready for the silo.

Soybeans are grown in the south-west, often in conjunction with corn. The two are natural partners, since soybeans can be sown after the corn yet can be harvested before the corn is ripe. But soybeans have not spread far afield, because their yield quickly decreases and other crops are more attractive. Farms in Eastern Ontario grow mustard.

The tobacco crop is restricted to the region centred on Norfolk county and pockets in the surrounding area, each distinguished by sandy soil with good drainage. Almost all the crop is destined to be 'flue-cured' (artificially dried in kilns), then processed as cigarette tobacco for the home market and for export.

Tobacco seedlings are nursed in greenhouses, then transplanted into open fields late in May or early in June. The industry is chiefly labour-intensive, and the crop needs constant attention until it is ready for harvesting in August. Leaves are picked as they mature from the bottom up, until in the end only the stalk remains.

Vegetables are grown in 'muck' soils, the residue of drained bogs rich in decomposed vegetation. Especially important are Holland Marsh in Simcoe county, Thetford Marsh in Lambton, which is a dried-up lake bed, and an area in Kent county. The muck soils support big crops of carrots, tomatoes, onions, celery, and lettuce, while potatoes, sweet corn, and peas are generally grown on standard soils.

For six months of the year Ontario's weather makes outdoor vegetable farming impossible. Some producers use greenhouses to produce year-round tomatoes, cucumbers, lettuce, and other crops. South-western Ontario also supports important commercial crops of ornamental flowers.

starts growing again and can be harvested in August. If the crop is lost in the winter, the farmer has time to plough again in the spring and sow oats or barley or some other summer crop. However, Ontario oats and barley amount to only a small fraction of annual cereal output.

FRUIT AND WINE

The showpiece of Ontario agriculture is the fruit-growing area of the Niagara Peninsula, especially famous for apples, grapes, and peaches. But other regions contribute too, and Ontario's fruit farms produce nearly half of Canada's overall output.

Ontario's fruits are usually classified in four botanical groups. Tree varieties include core fruits, like apples and pears, and stone fruits, like peaches, plums, and cherries. Berries are typically grown on bushes, and include blackberries, blueberries, and grapes, but strawberries and raspberries are 'aggregates.'

Apple and pear production is spread throughout Southern Ontario, and was introduced by the Loyalists. In 1811 John McIntosh, a Scottish immigrant, found twenty wild apple trees on his land in Eastern Ontario. From these he developed the McIntosh apple, which today makes up nearly 50 per cent of Canada's crop.

In a traditional apple orchard, producers favour wide-spaced trees which are allowed to develop naturally. But in the interests of greater productivity (and easier harvesting) the old method has given way to closer plantings of smaller-sized trees. So far there is no mechanized improvement of traditional hand-picking from ladders, with care taken not to bruise the fruit.

Peaches are more delicate than the core fruits, and are largely restricted to the Niagara Peninsula and the Lake Erie region. Several of the favourite varieties have been developed in Canada. As with all deciduous fruit trees (those which drop their leaves in fall), the farmer must observe a year-round cultivation cycle if he wants the best from his crop.

Following the harvest, he prunes the trees to give them the right shape — not too tall, allowing adequate space for light and air and access for spraying and picking. Besides, this helps induce the tree to put its efforts into producing fruit rather than growing new branches.

From the time the first 'green-tip' buds appear on the farmer's deciduous trees — in this case apples — he applies a variety of chemical sprays, including fertilizers, trace elements, and pest and insect poisons.

Wine grapes are picked by a mechanical harvester when they are ready to be transported to the winery for crushing and further processing.

An unusual means of harvesting is the mobile platform used by strawberry-pickers.

Ontario cherry farmers use an elaborate 'shaker' platform to dislodge fruit from trees.

In spring the trees burst into blossom. When the first green-tip buds appear, the farmer applies fertilizer sprays, herbicides, and insecticides, and as the fruitlets form, he culls unwanted tips to encourage heavy growth in what remains. From this point the fruit is allowed to mature until ready for picking, probably late in August.

Grapevine cultivation follows the same general pattern, except that growth is more luxuriant and must be pruned more drastically to maintain a consistent crop. The Niagara Peninsula produces both table grapes and the more prolific wine grapes. With table varieties the chief criterion is appearance, and bunches should be thinned as they grow. This care is not necessary with wine grapes, for here the major consideration is sugar content. The harvested grapes are trucked to a winery where they are crushed. The juice is pumped to fermentation tanks where yeast is introduced and its gradual transformation into wine takes place.

In the past Ontario wine-farmers have grown 'labrusca' varieties, best suited to the production of dessert wines like sherry and port. But a major transformation is under way as they replant vineyards with European-style 'vinifera' cultivars ideal for table wines, which have become more popular in Canada.

Wine-grape production lends itself to mechanical harvesting, and so do other forms of fruit farming. Cherries are shaken from their trees and collected by the same machine. Strawberry-pickers lie prone on mobile platforms to pick the delicate fruit grown on farms in the Niagara region.

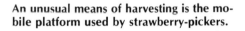

CROWN TIMBER

All but one-tenth of Ontario's productive forest is Crown timber, owned and managed by the provincial government in the public interest. Most of it is harvested and processed by private corporations operating under licence in specified areas.

Before 1900 logging companies were permitted to export whatever timber they cut, on payment of a 'stumpage' fee, which was calculated on the quantity involved. Pines from the Ottawa and St. Lawrence valleys were shipped to Europe, and later those within reach of the Great Lakes were ferried over to sawmills in Michigan.

It seemed the supply could never be exhausted, and in any case logging operations opened land for agriculture and settlement. There was a further bonus when companies began exporting pulpwood to the United States — until political stirrings in Ontario urged the provincial government to promote Ontario forest industries.

The government could do nothing about land owned privately, but in 1898 Ontario was the first province to ban the export of unsawn timber cut on Crown land. Two years later a law prohibited the export of unprocessed pulpwood cut on Crown land. Those were the first steps taken towards conserving Canada's forests.

Of course the steps were taken late. The white pine had all but disappeared. Besides, much of the land so optimistically cleared for agriculture had proved disappointing and lay deserted. In 1908 Canada's first nursery was established at St. Williams, close to Lake Erie, to supervise reforestation of the surrounding farmland with seedlings.

With the principle established, the government soon encouraged companies cutting Crown timber to monitor natural regeneration and take action where needed. Nine more nurseries were established to help them. Then, in 1962, the government made itself responsible for all forest regeneration on Crown land.

In view of the lack of reforestation in the past, it might seem that the best way to protect a forest would be to stop harvesting altogether. But that is not so. Trees grow as people do, particularly when they are young, and if left to themselves they become old and infirm and eventually die of old age. It makes sense to utilize their wood as soon as the trees mature and allow new ones to grow in their place. Normally the forest regenerates itself, but where it needs assistance, forest 'silviculturists' plant seedlings and nurse them to maturity. The expected rotation cycle of softwoods is, in most cases, 80 to 100 years.

Today the corporations harvesting Crown timber must respect each area's 'sustained yield' — in other words, they may cut no more timber each year than the forest can produce as its annual

An Indian tree-planting crew systematically plants young white spruce in an area cleared of timber. The shoots are drawn from government nurseries, where they have been raised from seed.

tions. Most of these agreements concern northern softwood. Before they may begin harvesting, companies must obtain government approval of their plans for long-term, medium-term, and immediate operations in the forest.

Each company pays stumpage on the wood it cuts, which is calculated on volume and also on species. Besides this, it pays a standard annual 'forest protection and management' fee, which helps balance the costs of the province's airborne fire-detection patrol and of action taken against disease and insects.

In the case of Algonquin Provincial Park, the government has taken over responsibility for the forest harvest and supplies specific timber to the local timber industry for processing as lumber or veneer products. A Crown corporation (the Algonquin Forest Authority) co-ordinates the many programs operating in the park — not forestry alone, but also recreation, wildlife conservation, and preservation of the natural environment.

This is a good example of the multi-purpose use of Crown forests now encouraged throughout the province. Several of the private corporations recognize this goal, and through their forest access roads and specially established campsites, they enable visitors to take full advantage of Ontario's most important renewable resource.

One great menace of the forest industry is wildfire. Air-borne patrols watch for outbreaks, and specially equipped aircraft can help contain it, while ground crews make their way to the area to bring it under control.

Nurseries run by the provincial government ship millions of seedlings to forest areas each year.

growth. They must allow for possible damage by fire, wind, insects, and disease, which could drastically revise the annual allowable cut.

Some of the harvesting of Crown land is carried out by private corporations on short-term agreements or by contractors brought in by the government. But two-thirds is in the hands of private corporations holding long-term agreements, usually granted for twenty-one years and subject to strict condi-

Spiked chains are dragged over ground cleared of timber, to expose mineral soil by 'scarification.' This process assists natural regeneration by surrounding trees, and where necessary regeneration is assisted by government foresters.

LOGGING CAMPS

Fifty years ago Ontario's lumberjacks rose long before first light, laboured until dark, and were expected to be in their bunks with lamps out at nine o'clock in the evening. They thrived on a cookhouse fare of pork and beans washed down with a dish of tea.

Recruited in September, the lumberjacks worked until the next spring — six days a week, with their chief pleasure the free night each Saturday. This was an occasion for all-night poker, or all-male square-dancing to fiddle and harmonica, or solo ballads passed on from generation to generation.

Everyone slept in the bunkhouse, the biggest cabin in the camp. Along its side walls ran two tiers of double bunks, all within reach of a stove in the middle. There were small skylights for ventilation. Men washed in ice-cold water, and each evening after supper they took turns sharpening axes on the camp's grindstones.

Log-cutters worked in gangs of six. Two men felled the trees and cut them

The boreal forest, which stretches across Northern Ontario, supports a chain of pulp and paper mills. This one is at Port Arthur, part of Thunder Bay.

Today's logging camps are far more comfortable than they were in the great days of the old-time lumberjacks. Some camps are fixed, like this one. Others consist of mobile trailers which can be moved on as required.

The Industry

In the hardwood forests, trees are cut selectively, as in earlier days. But in the north the old-style 'clear-cutting,' by which continuous hectares were stripped in hundreds, has given way to 'modified cutting,' by which tracts are gradually harvested in strips over many years. This method helps the forest to regenerate itself, section by section.

In Ontario, softwood harvesting is by volume about four times as great as hardwood production — which means that many more trees must be handled, considering the smaller size of the softwood tree. Some pulp and paper mills have integrated their operations by adding a sawmill at the pulp and paper site to produce lumber.

By value, Ontario's most important wood product is newsprint, which amounts to about 25 per cent of Canadian output. Most goes to the United States. There is major production of fine papers, kraft (wrapping and packaging) papers, and wood pulp. Most pulp and paper mills are sited in Northern Ontario, near their sources of raw materials.

Sawmills in Ontario produce 40 per cent of Canada's hardwood lumber (mostly in the south), and 6 per cent of softwood lumber. Wood residue from the sawmills, whether hardwood or softwood, now plays a major part in pulp and paper production, along with conventional softwood chips. In all there are more than 800 wood-mills of various kinds in Ontario, and forest products processing provides employment for nearly 80 000 people.

into 5 m lengths, using axes and a cross-cut saw. Two men made up the bucking crew, trimming logs of limbs and knots and stacking the 'slash.' The third pair cut a road for a teamster's horses, which hauled the logs to an iced 'skidway.'

That was the shape of Ontario logging until the early 1930s, particularly in the hardwood forests of the south. During the mid-1940s machines were introduced to improve productivity, most of them adapted from agriculture and the construction industry. But the greatest single advance was the introduction of the power chainsaw.

Today machines are designed to carry out the forest harvest. The most advanced grips a tree along its whole length, then shears its limbs, tops it, snips the bottom of its trunk, and stacks it as a log, all in one swift operation. The mechanical harvester is used extensively in the uniform boreal pulpwood forests of the north.

There have been great changes in loggers' living styles. Gone are the old communal bunkhouses. Instead loggers often sleep in modern trailers, which can be moved on as required. Pork and beans have given way to varied meals cooked on prime facilities, and many camps include recreation rooms equipped with colour television.

But the biggest change is in loggers' mobility. In nearly every case they can drive to the nearest town on weekends and perhaps live at home throughout the week. The old-style logger was a manual labourer, but today's is a technician — versed not only in good forestry practice, but also in operating and maintaining the complex machinery now utilized.

Ontario's forest industry employs some 10 000 people in harvesting trees, compared with 60 000 in Canada as a whole. A rising proportion are women, who have long been engaged in camp cookhouses but are now at work in the bush as well. Today's loggers work year-round and not merely through the winter, as in the past.

The logging industry was revolutionized by the introduction of the power chainsaw, particularly in the 1950s. Each logger owns his own, and it is the most important tool of his trade.

33

FISH AND FUR

Fifty years ago it seemed that Ontario's trappers and fishermen could never run short of good catches. But over-exploitation of the beaver and a parasitic invasion of the Great Lakes placed both industries in serious trouble.

As regards fishing, the invading parasite was the sea lamprey, a kind of eel which attached itself to live fish by rasping a hole in their flesh. It sucks out their blood and body fluids. After causing havoc in Lake Ontario, the lamprey reached the northern lakes by way of the Welland Canal, bypassing Niagara Falls.

In earlier days the northern lakes teemed with such species as lake trout, whitefish, lake herring, and lake sturgeon. Over two decades these were progressively eliminated, lake by lake. In 1955 Canada and the United States formed the Great Lakes Fishing Commission to cope with the menace by systematically weeding out the lamprey.

Provincial fish hatcheries do what they can to restore the lake trout and whitefish of the Great Lakes. But the character of the commercial fishery has changed profoundly. It is centred on Lake Erie as before, for it alone among the Great Lakes is shallow and relatively warm. The catch consists largely of yellow perch (caught in gill nets) and smelt.

Ironically, these species were formerly considered of little commercial value. Indeed the smelt was another interloper — a small seawater species which normally visited fresh water only to spawn, but which suddenly thrived in the Great Lakes after being introduced deliberately. Now it is trawled in Lake Erie in great quantities.

Lake Erie produces about 70 percent of Ontario's catch, and production there and in the other Great Lakes is slowly recovering. In the past there has been commercial fishing in many of Ontario's 'inland' lakes too, but in some areas this has been suspended following the detection of high levels of mercury pollution in fish caught there.

The problems which overwhelmed Ontario's trappers in the 1920s and 1930s were largely of their own making. During the Depression many more than usual tried to earn their way in the

The trapper sets most of his traps underwater, since he usually aims to snare aquatic creatures like the beaver and muskrat, which between them account for some 90 per cent of his catch.

The chief target of the Ontario trapper is the beaver, which survived a dangerous period of over-trapping in the 1930s. It has since recovered its previous strong position as a result of careful conservation.

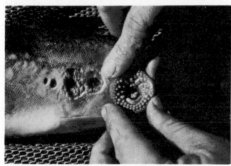

The bane of fishing in the lower Great Lakes is the sea lamprey, an eel-like parasite which attaches itself to other fish by its sucker-like mouth.

forest, and their efforts seriously depleted the beaver, which had always been the mainstay of the fur trade.

The provincial government imposed closed seasons to allow the beaver to recover, and in one instance extended the closed season for several years. But it was difficult to enforce, and when it was lifted, trappers were as ruthless as ever. More subtly, the government restricted professional trappers to their own registered traplines.

The effect was to encourage trappers to 'farm' their traplines, driving off predators and, indeed, rival trappers, and as far as possible conserving species by making sure that they were breeding and had enough to eat. The result is that Ontario's beaver population is as high as it has ever been, and other species are thriving too.

A trapline is an area of Crown land allotted to the particular trapper when he is granted his licence. It may range in size from a few square kilometres in favoured areas, to enormous tracts of the north. In either case the trapper pays a standard royalty on his catch, usually 5 per cent of the previous year's selling price.

Three types of trap are in common use, set either on land or underwater. The 'leghold' trap has been in use for many centuries, and catches the animal by the foot. The spring-released 'conibear' grabs the animal around the body. The 'snare' is a loop catching it around the neck or foot and holding it by a slip-knot.

Many species are trapped in Ontario, but aquatic creatures like the beaver and muskrat make up 90 per

Commercial fishing in Ontario is concentrated on Lake Erie, shallowest and warmest of the Great Lakes. This is a scene at Port Dover on the Erie shore, home of a trawler fleet that fishes for yellow perch and smelt, among other species.

cent of the catch. Year by year there are wide fluctuations in price, depending on demand. Otter, fisher, and arctic fox have been fashionable but have been eclipsed by lynx.

Overall, Ontario trappers provide more than a quarter of Canada's total catch of wild pelts. There has been a steady demand for wild mink, but most of it is satisfied by the many mink ranches in the province. These produce not only standard pelts, but also mutation types like platinum (*silverblu*) and pastel.

MINING

The rich base-metal potential of the Canadian Shield was recognized long before serious attempts were made to exploit it. But would-be developers were discouraged by lack of suitable transport and rewarding markets.

Significantly, the first discovery to produce an important mine was made by a blacksmith working in a Canadian Pacific Railway rock-blasting gang — Tom Flanagan, who in 1883 noticed rust marks in a cutting near what is now Sudbury. He probed the spot with a pick and uncovered glittering sulphide ores.

The ores were later found to contain rich proportions of copper and nickel and other minerals too. In the years that followed a number of base-metal mines were developed in the area, along the line of what proved to be an oval-shaped basin 60 km long and 27 km wide.

Remarkably similar circumstances surrounded the second major discovery in the Shield — the great silver deposits of Cobalt, in 1903. This time the Ontario government was building a railway north from North Bay. Two tie contractors looking for timber noticed a sulphide outcrop and sent samples to Montreal for analysis. The samples contained unprecedented grades of silver, and soon Cobalt was a thriving mining camp. Prospectors combed the area un-

Ag SILVER	Cu COPPER	Pt PLATINUM
Asb ASBESTOS	Fe IRON	S SULPHUR
Au GOLD	Gyp GYPSUM	U URANIUM
Co COBALT	Pb LEAD	Zn ZINC

Ontario's major mining centres, most of them exploiting the base-metal resources of the Canadian Shield.

Ore from the working face is transported to crushers by heavyweight load-haul-dumpers, which in many mines have replaced old-style underground railways.

til, in 1909, one slipped on a steep hillside near Porcupine Lake. His boot scraped the moss from a ledge of quartz, which he traced to a dome-shaped structure studded with gold.

In weeks prospectors were active throughout the Porcupine area and located half a dozen significant deposits. One camp was named after its developer, Noah Timmins of Cobalt. Other discoveries were at Larder Lake in 1906, around Kirkland Lake in 1912, and far to the west at Red Lake in 1925.

Meanwhile World War I encouraged a boom in base-metal production, not least at Wawa, which produced iron ore for a smelter in Sault Ste. Marie. There was a similar boost during World War II, and developers opened iron ore deposits at Atikokan in the far west. This operation involved draining Steep Rock Lake, which was 10 km wide.

But all this was mere prelude to the great boom in Ontario mining

Under Lake Huron near Goderich, miners quarry Canada's most extensive deposits of rock salt. The province uses quantities of it to dissolve snow in winter, but salt is used in many other ways; for example, as table salt following special refining. ▼

A basic tool of the miner is the compressed-air drill, here seen in action at the New Quirke uranium mine near Elliot Lake. The miner drills holes in a prearranged pattern and charges them with explosives to be detonated in sequence.

Open-pit mines consist of concentric 'benches' shelved back to eliminate cave-ins. This is the Steep Rock iron mine at Atikokan, where a lake was drained to allow access to the ore body.

recovery techniques, which make it possible to exploit lower grades of ore.

Not all of Ontario's minerals are drawn from the Canadian Shield. Southwestern Ontario still produces small quantities of natural gas and oil. Salt in the region is mined as rock or recovered from brine wells. The salt beds of Goderich are Canada's most extensive — 35 m deep and 80 km wide.

Other minerals exploited in Ontario include gypsum, which, like salt, is the product of evaporated seawater, and a range of structural materials, like building stone, sand, clay, and limestone for portland cement. However, taking all mineral production into account, Ontario trails Alberta in value of output because of the success of western oil.

On the other hand, Ontario leads Canada in nineteen categories of mineral production, notably nickel, copper, and zinc. Other categories are gold, silver, platinum, uranium, magnesium, cadmium, salt, and a range of structural materials.

which followed World War II. The 1950s saw the emergence of Manitouwadge, where deposits of copper, zinc, silver, and lead provoked a major rush to the wilderness to stake claims, and of Elliot Lake, a Z-shaped zone rich in uranium.

In the 1960s the original mines of the Porcupine were running out of gold, but considerable deposits of copper and zinc were found nearby. Since then other base-metal mines have commenced production, and among them several are mining iron ore. All use new

NICKEL CITY

The Sudbury basin, which provides so much of the world's nickel and copper, was created by a meteorite. So great was its impact that it shattered the earth's crust, allowing metal-bearing magma to squeeze up to the surface.

Before 1962 geologists assumed that Sudbury was the result of a volcano. But then a marine geologist, an American who had studied meteorite impact sites on the moon, surmised that the huge basin had had the same origin. He predicted that he would find 'shatter cones' — tiny fractures in the rock outside, pointing in like arrows. Sure enough he found them. It was a major feat of geological detective work and

has greatly helped geologists wanting to understand the Sudbury formation. Its ore body is best pictured as a web like a giant umbrella turned upside down. The edges are near the surface around the basin's rim, but the middle is too deep to be explored.

A bewildering range of mining techniques is employed at Sudbury. At one extreme is 'open-pit mining,' in which miners excavate from the surface; at the other is 'blasthole mining,' where immense vertical columns of ore are broken up in one blast, following the drilling of thousands of holes for the necessary explosives. The most common mining method is 'cut-and-fill.' Here

miners remove a slice of ore, then half-fill the cavity with waste materials to provide a working platform. They stand on this to mine the next slice. In this way they continue upwards for some 65 m, until they reach the next mining level.

The ore body is explored in advance by diamond drills, which probe down 1500 m or farther. To develop an underground mine, a vertical shaft is sunk through barren rock near the ore body. A double-decker cage delivers miners to the level where they are working, and two 'skips' will carry broken ore to the surface for processing.

From the shaft, miners tunnel a

'crosscut' to intersect the ore body at each level. At right angles to this they mine an 'access drive,' which follows the line of ore body. Levels are connected by a series of near-vertical 'raises' and 'ore passes,' through which ore falls to crushers at the mine bottom.

Miners normally work an eight-hour shift. Typical jobs include drilling the rock ready to insert blasting charges, and once the 'muck' has been blasted, removing it and hauling it to the nearest ore pass. In most Sudbury mines, muck is hauled in low-profile 'load-haul-dumpers' (LHDs) running on thick tires. For safety's sake, the roof of a section just blasted is 'scaled' to remove loose rock, then strengthened with long roofbolts and a steel mesh to prevent major bursts. No longer must the miner work in virtual darkness, since as far as possible, proper illumination is carried right up to the working face.

On the surface, broken ore is crushed again, then finely milled in large revolving cylinders which contain rods or balls. Water is added to produce a fine 'slurry,' in which form the ore is conveyed to 'flotation tables,' where particles containing metal are floated off in a chemical solution. At Sudbury this solution is adjusted to produce sulphide concentrates, which are predominantly either nickel or copper. As an extra refinement, iron sulphides are removed by means of metallic drums and are processed separately. Nickel and copper concentrates are forwarded to the smelter to be treated on separate circuits.

Nickel from Sudbury, along with a small quantity from Shebandowan, near Thunder Bay, accounts for about 75 per cent of Canada's production. Most of it is smelted and refined in Ontario. A small proportion is bought by Canadian manufacturers, notably steelmills, but the bulk is exported. The chief customer is the United States.

Sudbury has an undeserved reputation as a kind of no man's land in which no vegetation will grow. Instead, the town is blessed with many attractive spots, particularly near its lakes, which are popular with sailors and swimmers throughout summer.

As a safety measure, the roof of a section just blasted is scaled to remove loose rock, and then strengthened with long roofbolts and a steel mesh to eliminate major rockbursts. Here miners drill holes for the roofbolts.

PRECIOUS METALS

Platinum, gold, and silver are often called 'noble' metals, as distinct from 'base' metals. All three are found in Ontario, and in such quantity that the province is the world's leading source of silver and Canada's leading source of platinum and gold.

Ontario's silver was first noticed at Spar Island, south of Thunder Bay, in 1846. However, no mining was attempted until the discovery of a rich vein in 1866. This led to the development of several mines, including that on the tiny Silver Islet in Lake Superior, which commenced in 1868 and continued until 1884 when a winter storm flooded the workings.

There was further spasmodic mining near Thunder Bay, but nothing to compare with the operations which followed the discovery of Cobalt in 1903. The name sprang from the cobalt which accompanied the silver found in narrow veins only a few centimetres across, but extending long distances and contained in otherwise worthless rock. Miners learned lessons which later proved valuable as they moved to other mines. Cobalt is not referred to as 'the cradle of Canadian mining' for nothing. However, the silver boom might have ended more quickly without advances in metallurgy, which made it possible to utilize not silver alone, but cobalt too.

In recent years, however, the bulk of Ontario's silver production has come not from the silver mines, but from base-metals mines like those in Sudbury and the Kidd Creek mine near Timmins. Here silver emerges as a by-product of electrolytic zinc refining, making Kidd Creek the world's biggest single source.

Much of Ontario's gold is a by-product of the same processes. Rising production costs cut into the profits of the older gold mines, and when the gold price dives, those mining low-grade ores are faced with heavy losses. One by one they have been forced to close, and only two are sure to survive for many years to come.

But gold mines still function in each of the chief areas of discovery. There are mines at Timmins and at Porcupine Lake, around Kirkland Lake, and to the west near Red Lake. The biggest is the Kerr Addison mine at Larder Lake, where mercury plates and cyanide are used to separate the metal from accompanying impurities.

The Porcupine region still holds a number of small, operational gold mines, like Aunor, pictured here. Notice the slimes dam beyond the headgear, to which potentially poisonous slimes from the recovery process are drained of water and consolidated as waste.

Molten gold is poured in a mine smelthouse. The gold is recovered from its ore by complex smelting processes, in which the gold is dissolved and absorbed in a cyanide solution, then, after filtering, precipitated by the addition of zinc dust.

Mining on Silver Islet in Lake Superior began in 1864 and continued until 1884. Canada's most unusual ghost town survives as a memorial.

Cobalt, in north-eastern Ontario, is known as the cradle of Canada's mining industry, in that so many Canadian miners cut their teeth down the shafts of its silver mines. Most have been worked out, and only gaunt headframes survive to commemorate Cobalt's boom years at the beginning of the century.▼

Exploration for possible new deposits of precious metals continues but is very different from prospecting for base metals. Sulphide deposits of nickel, copper, and zinc can be detected by means of geophysical instruments which react to the iron usually accompanying them, but payable gold is normally on its own.

Instead, most notable gold deposits have been located by prospectors tramping the ground on foot, relying more on luck than on scientific investigation. Such prospectors may spot clues which lead them to outcrops on the surface, but those buried even centimetres deep may never be uncovered.

Though gold and silver are far from ugly sisters, it might appear that platinum is the Cinderella of noble metals. It is the rarest of the three so it is worth the most, yet somehow it has never acquired the glamorous image accorded to the others. Very few countries consider it worthy of its own hallmarks.

To make things more complicated, platinum is just one of a group of metals always found together — the others being palladium, ruthenium, rhodium, iridium, and osmium. They are referred to as the platinum group metals, and are recovered as by-products of nickel and copper refining at Sudbury.

COPPER AND ZINC

If the noble metals are sisters, then so are nickel, copper, and zinc. In Ontario copper sulphides are found by themselves or with nickel or zinc, but nickel and zinc sulphides are never found in combination.

The earliest record of copper in Ontario notes that in 1770 Jesuit missionaries experimented with copper on the shores of Lake Superior — that is, 'native' copper, existing as a metal in its own right. Indians worked copper to make tools and weapons more effective than stones and bones.

From 1847 immigrant Cornish miners worked copper in the Bruce mines of the Algoma district and processed it in Canada's first copper smelter. However, production was small and the mines were overshadowed by the discoveries at Sudbury in 1883. At first it was believed that the Sudbury ores contained only copper.

The next discovery of importance followed intensive prospecting by the Ontario government, which in 1931 noted sulphides near a lake named Manitouwadge. But the area was deep in the wilderness, and not until 1953 did local men encourage development of the copper-zinc deposits now mined as Geco and Willroy.

The success of Manitouwadge triggered a modern prospecting boom throughout Northern Ontario. At the forefront were loggers already stationed in the wilds. These men soon equipped themselves with geiger counters, following the rapid development of uranium deposits near by at Elliot Lake. But no fortunes were made.

A third major base-metal deposit came to light in 1964, following intensive aerial prospecting in the Timmins area. This was the Kidd Creek copper-zinc deposit, located under muskeg. The terrain posed major problems for the developers, in spite of six years of careful exploration.

Other base-metal mines have been opened, notably those at Ignace, northwest of Thunder Bay, which produce copper and zinc. In recent years Ontario's zinc production has amounted to more than 30 per cent of Canada's total and helps to make it the world's leading source.

In the recovery process, slurry from the mills is pumped to flotation tables — flat, shallow, open cells flooded with frothy chemical bubbles, which attract particles of metal and overflow into recovery channels.

The Kidd Creek copper-zinc deposit was located under muskeg near Timmins. It was discovered through aerial prospecting in 1964.

Far from ravaging tracts of open country for the resources they can produce, mining companies (and the provincial government) make sure that they disturb the environment as little as possible. This is the scene at the Geco copper and zinc mines of north-central Ontario.

Sudbury has a copper smelter and electrolytic refinery, and a nickel smelter and non-electrolytic refinery. Nickel is processed in Port Colborne on Lake Erie, and zinc at a smelter and electrolytic refinery in Timmins. Sulphide smelting eliminates waste materials by melting the concentrate and allowing metals to settle out.

The end product of the smelting process is a metal about 98 per cent pure. In electrolytic refining this is cast as 'anode plates' — flat sheets which are set in lead-lined tanks filled with a warm chemical solution. An electric current induces microscopic grains of metal to transfer to 'cathode' sheets facing the anodes. Impurities — including precious metals — are later collected from the solution.

Some of Ontario's copper goes forward to local manufacturers, but the major share is destined for the international export markets. Here Canadian copper meets stiff competition from producers in Chile, Peru, Zaire, and Zambia. Unfortunately the copper price fluctuates wildly. In four of the chief exporting countries, copper is the responsibility of governments which cannot afford to restrict production. The international zinc market is more stable, dominated by private enterprise in Canada, Australia, and Peru.

STEELTOWN

Around the western end of Lake Ontario is the succession of rich industrial communities known as the 'Golden Horseshoe.' It stretches from Oshawa to Niagara-on-the-Lake and includes Toronto, but it is centred on Hamilton.

Tucked away under the Niagara Escarpment and off natural transport routes, Hamilton was a slow starter in the early days of Upper Canada. However, in the 1850s the Great Western Railway was persuaded to route its track through Hamilton rather than along the top of the escarpment, and a few years later it built its main workshops there.

That gave Hamilton its start as an engineering centre. Iron foundries and machine shops came into production and the population boomed. However, at first there was no progress towards establishing an integrated steel industry of the type then emerging in American cities. It was cheaper to import tariff-free pig iron from Scotland.

Then, in 1879 the federal government imposed a heavy tariff on imported pig iron, hoping to encourage the development of a Canadian industry. The move favoured Nova Scotia, where local supplies of iron ore were readily available. Hamilton mills were seriously disadvantaged, and a production slump ensued.

But local entrepreneurs soon persuaded American concerns to open a steelworks in Hamilton, utilizing iron ore shipped from Lake Superior via Sault Ste. Marie and the newly modified Welland Canal, which could now accommodate larger ships. Limestone was in plentiful supply on the escarpment, and coking coal could be brought from the south.

And that was the start of the steelmaking industry for which Hamilton is famous today. The two great integrated steelworks in the city produce about 60 per cent of Canada's steel requirements. These are the raw materials of scores of industries based in the Golden Horseshoe and elsewhere in Central Canada.

Steel-making is a series of operations not unlike the smelting and refining of non-ferrous metals. Steel is an alloy of iron and carbon (usually only 1 to 1.6 per cent), each of which is brittle in itself but superbly strong in combination.

The main control pulpit of a rod mill, with the complex control system miniaturized so that all can be controlled by one operator.

Molten steel being poured during foundry operations at a Hamilton steelmill. ▼

44

Despite its hardworking image as Ontario's most concentrated centre of heavy industry, Hamilton is a pleasant city. These are the Royal Botanical Gardens.

The pride of Hamilton is Dundurn Castle, built by Allan MacNab, who intended it to be the finest building in Canada. MacNab was Hamilton's first lawyer, and after taking a leading role in driving William Lyon Mackenzie from Upper Canada, he entered politics. In his later years he brought the railway to Hamilton, ensuring its superiority over neighbouring communities.

The pig iron contains a high proportion of carbon drawn from the coke, and this must be reduced to produce steel. Most methods use extreme temperatures and blasts of oxygen to burn off the carbon as carbon monoxide. Normally a small quantity of scrap steel is added to speed this oxidation.

At this stage special metals may be added to produce steel alloys. These include nickel steel and stainless steel (containing 12 to 18 per cent chromium and 8 per cent nickel); stellite steel used in high speed tools; vanadium steel, which is especially long-lasting; and wolfram steel, which remains hard at high temperatures.

From the furnace the steel is 'teemed' (poured) into ingot moulds, then trucked to the rolling mills. If the steel is to be made into sheets or other flat products, the ingot is rolled as a rectangular slab so that it is ready to undergo further rolling in the plate mill. Initial rolling is hot, but later cold rolling is more precise.

If the steel is required in the form of bars, wire rods, or such products, the ingot is shaped as a 'bloom,' which is roughly square in cross-section, then is further reduced in size to become a 'billet.' In one process billets can be cast continuously six at a time, using molten metal directly from the furnace and bypassing the ingot stage.

Besides hot- and cold-rolling steel, a third important technique is 'casting,' in which the molten steel is poured directly into the mould shape required. Other available techniques are refinements of these — for instance, electrolytic tin-plating, where a coating of tin is applied, and 'galvanizing,' which is bathing steel in zinc.

The Hamilton steelworks support industrial enterprises ranging from the giants of the transportation industry — particularly automobile and rolling-stock manufacturers — to construction and the appliance and domestic hardware industry. Many of these are based in Hamilton, Burlington, and the surrounding region.

Small quantities of other metals may be introduced to make alloys with special advantages.

The first step is to make pig iron through a kind of smelting. Measured quantities of iron ore pellets (with major impurities already removed), coke (coal pre-roasted to burn more effectively), and limestone (as flux) are fed into a blast-furnace. 'Pig iron' is so named because of the shape of moulds once used to cast the molten iron.

AUTOMOBILES

Canada's motor vehicle and automotive parts industries are firmly rooted in south-western Ontario. A contributing factor is the big local consumer market, but the chief reason is the proximity of Detroit in Michigan.

Inevitably, the United States' motor-town has overshadowed Canadian production since the early days. In 1903, Henry Ford established his factory in Detroit and devised his pioneer mass-production techniques. Within a year a group of Canadians arranged to assemble Ford cars across the river in Walker-ville, now part of Windsor.

The advantage of the scheme to Ford was that the Canadians enjoyed tariff advantages throughout the British Empire and in other countries too. The group was granted a franchise to make Ford cars for export anywhere in the Empire except in Britain. They were soon launched on production of the

A relatively late stage on the assembly line — the body is united with its motor.

Substructures are assembled independently, then incorporated with the vehicle body on the assembly line. ▼

Model C, and later of the Model T.

Meanwhile there was competition from manufacturers in Oshawa. The McLaughlin Carriage Company had been established there in 1876 to make carriages and sleighs, but in 1907 it began making automobiles with Buick engines imported from Michigan. From 1915 the McLaughlins also made the Chevrolet, which soon became the Model T's great rival.

In 1918 McLaughlins was taken over by the United States' General Motors, but like Ford, General Motors was producing cars for the Canadian and Empire markets. Several much smaller manufacturers were in the field too. Until the Depression, Canada was the world's number two automotive manufacturer and remained important until long after World War II.

But in the 1950s the situation changed dramatically. Many of the countries to which Canada had exported now had automotive industries of their own. At home, Canadians began buying smaller, lower-priced cars imported from Britain and Europe. Canadians were buying 7.5 per cent of cars sold in North America, but were making only 4 per cent profit.

Another serious problem was that with lessening production, both assembly plants and manufacturers had to lay off workers. At the same time Canadian-made cars included a high proportion of components imported from the United States, which adversely affected the trade balance between the countries.

The government appointed a royal commission of inquiry. Its purpose was to find a way to protect and, if possible, increase job opportunities, but without driving car prices to impossible levels. The commission returned with a radical, imaginative solution: mass-produce

Teams of auto workers carry out carefully scheduled assembly routines as the vehicle moves slowly along the assembly line.

motor parts in Canada for the whole North American market and insist that they be taken in exchange for imported parts.

Economists and politicians bridled, for the proposal ran counter to all trade patterns affecting the two countries. But the industry itself was in favour of the arrangement — not least because the 'big four' North American manufacturers shared nearly all the market between them. In 1965 the two countries signed the 'Auto Pact.'

The pact sets conditions to protect Canada, but its broad effect is to allow 'original manufacturers' to import and export parts and vehicles duty free, provided the eventual market is fairly distributed between them. Rather than duplicate assembly lines, a manufacturer can mass-produce for all North America in one location.

In practice this might work as follows: manufacturer A can produce its whole North American output of Model L in Windsor, Model M in Detroit, and Model N in Chicago, to be distributed as required between the United States and Canada. Windshield wipers for all three models might be made by an independent components manufacturer in Hamilton.

So far the arrangement has worked well, and it has achieved its objectives. Canadian components manufacturers now mass-produce for all North America, and vehicle manufacturers are busier than ever before. Indeed, new vehicles and automotive parts have overtaken pulp and paper and agricultural products as Canada's chief exports.

The Industry

Canada's motor vehicle and components industries employ roughly similar numbers but differ greatly in organization. Motor vehicle manufacturers mass-produce and are enormous companies. Most have wholly owned subsidiaries to mass-produce components. But independent parts manufacturers tend to specialize, and they are usually quite small.

The 'big four' Canadian vehicle manufacturers are based in Ontario — General Motors in Oshawa, Ford in Oakville and St. Thomas, Chrysler in Windsor, and American Motors in Brampton. In addition, there are two major truck-building concerns, International Harvester in Chatham and Mack Trucks in Oakville.

On average, a vehicle consists of 15 000 separate components. Most parts manufacturers are located in the south-west, close to the assembly plants they supply, whether they are in Ontario or Michigan. Many draw steel from mills in Hamilton. Synthetic rubber for tires, fanbelts, and such items is supplied by petrochemical plants in Sarnia.

MANUFACTURING

Ontario is Canada's industrial heart. This is due not so much to primary industries like mining and forestry, as to secondary activities like manufacturing and construction. In these secondary categories Ontario stands far in advance of all other provinces.

As regards manufacturing, comparative economic importance is calculated in terms of 'value added' by the manufacturing process. In Canada's case, roughly four out of five dollars of this extra value is generated in the central provinces — more than 50 per cent in Ontario and nearly 30 per cent in Quebec. British Columbia, in third place, provides less than 10 per cent.

By its nature, however, the secondary sector resists sharp definition. In its widest sense, it takes in all processing of materials beyond their raw state — including pulp and paper mills, but probably not smelters or refineries. It extends to establishments like automobile assembly plants, which collate thousands of parts manufactured elsewhere.

For statistical purposes the manufacturing industry is divided into some twenty categories on a product basis — food and beverages, machinery, furniture, textiles, commercial printing, and so on. But each of these is only a loose grouping of elements which may have very little in common.

Instead, connections between manufacturers are more tangled. Even a simple final product may involve the operations of scores of plants. Any plastics components will probably have originated as ethylene, a by-product of oil refining that is later processed as raw material to be melted and blown or compressed into appropriate moulds.

Any metals involved may have been processed in four or five successive plants before reaching their final form, as may textiles. Even after the product has been assembled, it must be packaged, which introduces a range of fresh plants into the cycle, including pulp and paper mills, glass plants, can and cellulose manufacturers, and commercial printers.

Each operation is dependent on its suppliers of raw materials, its power supply, and those who service its machinery. Not surprisingly, it prefers to be as close to them as possible. At the same time it prefers to be close to its customers, whether they are other man-

Oil refineries and associated petrochemical works line the St. Clair river at Sarnia, the gateway to Lake Huron.

The blades of an industrial gas turbine being inspected.

development. These areas are fully serviced, but where possible they are kept separate from residential neighbourhoods. Environmental controls are exercised so strictly that often industrial communities are as clean as any other, but municipalities take no chances.

Some plants are enormous, employing many thousands and possibly maintaining production in continuous shifts to make full use of premises and equipment. But the majority are relatively small, employing fewer than one hundred people and often no more than one or two dozen. In the long run they are the backbone of the economy.

There have been efforts at the federal level to decentralize industry from the population centres and to spread its benefits more evenly. In Ontario much of the north and all of the east is relatively undeveloped. Valuable incentives offered at federal, provincial, and municipal levels encourage industries to move to these regions.

ufacturers or commercial distributors.

This is why industries tend to congregate close to their markets — and in Ontario that means Toronto and its surrounding centres. It is estimated that one-third of Canada's consumer market lies within 160 km of central Toronto, so inevitably that is the chief focus of industrial development.

Many municipal and regional authorities zone special areas for industrial

An automatic cutting machine is tested at a metal fabricating plant in Mississauga, the sprawling community west of Metropolitan Toronto.

Ontario's shipbuilding and repair industry is less well known than other manufacturing industries but has been significant since the opening of the St. Lawrence Seaway. These are the dry dock facilities at Port Weller, near St. Catharines.

Improved processing and packaging methods have resulted in an expanding variety of sausage products in Canada. Here smoked sausages emerge from processing in a meat packhouse.

High quality corn cobs are checked for defects in a vegetable processing plant before they are packed and frozen. ▼

FOOD PROCESSING

A key sector of the manufacturing industry is concerned with processing foods and beverages. Individual operations include meat packing, flour milling, fruit and vegetable canning and freezing, oilseed processing, baking, brewing, and distilling.

By Canadian law, all meat products are subject to rigorous government inspection — federal if they are to be sold outside the province in which they have been processed, and provincial if they are to be sold inside. Ontario packers process a range of cattle, hogs, calves, and poultry, along with frozen cuts, and develop products as varied as sausages and meat loaves.

The milling industry processes grain of all kinds — wheat, oats, barley, rye, and corn — whether grown in Ontario or shipped from the western provinces. Wheat is processed chiefly as baking flour (for bread) or cake flour (for cookies and cake), though some is processed especially for Italian-style pasta products.

Several industries are directly dependent on mills for their raw materials, notably bakeries, cookie manufacturers, and cereal producers. They use a wide range of techniques to produce special effects, particularly as consumers have grown more aware of nutritional values and favour simplicity.

Besides flour products, Ontario mills produce quantities of animal and poultry feed, particularly from corn. In addition, many are involved in oilseed processing, which is closely allied with milling. Oilseeds are used to make animal feeds and vegetable cooking oils, and are the chief ingredient of margarine.

Inevitably, margarine manufacturers are locked in combat with their rivals, the butter producers, who utilize an important proportion of the province's dairy production. But most of it is absorbed by fluid milk producers, who are obliged, under strict government control, to dispose of bacteria by pasteurization.

A quantity of industrial milk is used to make cheese, one of Ontario's oldest-established industries. A number of cheese varieties are produced, but the chief product is Canadian Cheddar. Some milk is concentrated (condensed) or powdered, and some fresh milk is processed as cottage cheese or cultured as yogurt.

The vegetable industry is centred in south-western Ontario, since processors like to be close to the farms that supply them. The processors give instructions to contracted farmers so that they can supply the exact quantity of vegetables required, and when harvested these are rushed to the plant to be cleaned, cut, pressed, or cooked.

Plants normally specialize in freezing or canning, which are equally effective with most vegetables. Fruit processors, however, prefer canning. A major proportion of the 'fruit' crop is tomatoes, and much of it is destined to be pressed as juice or processed as ketchup.

Ontario has to import a number of key commodities, though they may be further processed locally. One case is citrus fruit (mostly from Florida and California), and another is rice (from the Orient). But the most important is sugar, for only a fraction of the province's requirements can be met by Canadian-produced sugar beets.

Instead, semi-processed sugar cane is imported from the West Indies and South Africa, to be refined locally. Before the opening of the St. Lawrence Seaway, nearly all of eastern Canada's sugar was refined in Montreal. But now there are two refineries in Ontario, at Toronto and Oshawa, which are served directly by ocean freighter.

The raw materials of beverages like coffee, tea, and cocoa have to be imported too. For example, cocoa is made from cacao beans, which are also the basis of chocolate. Most tea is bagged; most coffee beans are blended and processed as instant coffee; most soft drinks are carbonated mixtures of water and sweetened concentrate.

Ontario's beer, whether ale or lager, is brewed from malt made from selected Canadian barley, pure water, hops from British Columbia, and sometimes small quantities of other ingredients like rice or corn. Malt is the basis of the brew, hops add flavour, but the key to the process is the addition of yeast, which produces fermentation.

The most famous product of Ontario's distilleries is Canadian rye whisky — though its chief ingredient is normally corn. However, its quality is none the

By federal law, meat destined for interprovincial or export trade must be processed in approved establishments under the supervision of government veterinary inspectors. Meat is inspected before, during, and after slaughter, and products meeting the required official standards are stamped 'Canada Approved' or the newer 'Canada.'

Pet food is a valuable sector of the food and beverages industry. Here burgers for dogs are packaged for the market.

worse for that, provided that scientific distilling is matched by conscientious blending. Other products distilled in Ontario include brandy, rum, gin, vodka, and a range of liqueurs.

Modern architectural standards in Toronto and elsewhere in Ontario are high. Among the many showpieces is the Toronto City Hall, designed by Viljo Revell and completed in the 1960s.

CONSTRUCTION

In some listings construction is treated as a service industry, but really it is a producer, in that it creates new physical assets. In terms of contribution to the gross national product, construction is Canada's biggest single industry.

Also, construction is probably more diverse than any other single industrial category, even food and beverages. Most of its products are one-of-a-kind, and range from chemical plants to office blocks and from bridges to schools. The materials and processes it uses are as wide-ranging as its products.

One way of classifying construction projects is to refer to their end purpose. Are they designed for people to live in, for people to use, or as an end in themselves? One major category is residential building, whether for single families or for a number of families at once (blocks of apartments, townhouses, and condominiums).

A second group includes institutional, commercial, and industrial developments — hospitals, schools, office blocks, stores, factories, and so on. Buildings like these will be used more extensively than residential units, and this must be reflected in their design and in the materials that go into them.

The third major category is more wide-ranging than the other two put together — the field of heavy engineering, which takes in road-building, pipe-laying, dam construction, bridge-building, and other activities. They include the steel construction in refineries, power projects, steelworks, and other such developments.

Most projects involve a three-way relationship between the developer (who hopefully knows what he wants), the architect and consulting engineer (who translate his wishes into plans), and the general contractor (who undertakes to carry the plans into action, with or without the help of specialist sub-contractors).

A major project involves sophisticated planning by the general contractor. In the case of a highrise apartment building or an office block, the contracting firm would normally first prepare the site, carrying out the necessary excavation, and driving reinforced concrete

piles down to bedrock to strengthen the foundation.

From this point the building progresses upwards — perhaps around an elevator core constructed first, so that it can support the overhead gantry cranes used to lift concrete and other materials to the working floors. Structural steelwork will probably be erected by specialist sub-contractors.

As the building progresses, the contractor calls in appropriate sub-contractors, probably in three categories — mechanical (to install plumbing, heating, and ventilation), electrical, and finishing (plastering and painting). On a highrise project they may work a floor or two below the contractor's personnel as they move up the building.

Besides actual construction operations, the contractor must take account of the materials required. On a typical project they might be drawn from scores of suppliers. They must be ordered well ahead of the time they will be needed, to allow the supplier to manufacture them.

The contracting firm is normally paid in monthly instalments in terms of the work it has done. The developer will probably have appointed the architect or consulting engineer to oversee each phase of the construction project as it advances, to make sure that all stages are completed in terms of the conditions in the contract.

In Ontario, all construction projects are subject to the strict provisions of the Ontario Building Code, introduced in 1976 to take the place of codes previously operated by individual municipalities. The code covers quality and safety aspects of buildings, and only when projects comply with these conditions are appropriate building permits issued.

Modern construction methods utilizing steel and concrete make for swift progress from the foundation up. Advances in concrete technology mean that construction can continue even during winter months.

As a building rises floor by floor, sub-contractors move in to install plumbing, heating, ventilation, and electrical systems, and to finish the building with plaster and paint.

Toronto workers joined in a national day of protest against wage and price controls on October 14, 1976. This is part of the crowd that gathered outside the Ontario parliament buildings.

Each year Ontario workers celebrate Labour Day, a civic holiday, with parades and rallies. Here a contingent of steel workers parade through downtown Toronto.

When even conciliation attempts fail, the workers have the right to strike and the employers have the right to lock them out. Here members of a newspaper typographical union picket the newspaper's offices on being locked out by their employers. ▼

LABOUR RELATIONS

Like other provinces, Ontario has extensive legislation covering the responsibilities of employers and the rights of employees. In particular, careful provisions govern the activities of trade unions, which, in turn, affect the whole work force.

Before 1872, Canadian trade unions were organized on an informal basis. Unions were legal, but conspiracy to disrupt trade was not. Then a union of printers in Toronto went on strike against local newspaper publishers. George Brown, the publisher of the *Globe*, laid charges against them on the grounds of conspiracy.

There had been a similar case in 1854, when Brown had won. But this time John A. Macdonald saw an opportunity to embarrass Brown, who was his chief political rival. He introduced legislation in the Dominion Parliament which repealed the old laws on conspiracy, thus recognizing Canadian workers' rights to form unions and use them to better their situation.

That position has been maintained to the present, though due to court decisions, labour affairs are now chiefly a provincial responsibility rather than a federal one. No more than 5 per cent of the Ontario labour force is under federal jurisdiction; for example, workers in such fields as interprovincial transportation and communications.

A group of workers wanting to form a union first invites applications from those who will be concerned. They must pay some kind of initiation fee to indicate their seriousness, as required by the province's labour laws. When a majority has joined, the group applies to the Labour Relations Board for certification.

This is the crucial process by which the province gives its blessing to the union as representative of the majority, and therefore empowers it to deal with management on the group's behalf. This takes the form of collective bargaining, in which union representatives and management meet to negotiate a contract.

The union approaches management with the proposals that it wants incorporated in the eventual contract. These will certainly include such matters as wages and hours to be worked, but in addition they will probably cover vacations, pensions, medical insurance, seniority provisions governing promotions, and a grievance procedure.

Bargaining can be slow because the union's proposals may be met by counter-proposals from management. But if all points are agreed to mutual satisfaction, they are incorporated in the contract, which covers employment conditions in that particular company for a specified period — normally one, two, or three years.

Where the parties cannot agree, the next stage is the appointment of a conciliation officer from the provincial Department of Labour. If he fails to bring about agreement, the matter goes before a conciliation board, normally consisting of three people — appointees of the company and the union, and a third person selected by them.

The board does not arbitrate, but instead offers recommendations to each side. If these terms are not acceptable, then the union has the right to strike — on the principle that the employer needs the workers' labour and that is all they have to bargain with. Conversely, the employer has the right to deprive them of work through a lock-out.

Once a contract is signed, strikes and lock-outs are illegal for its duration. Any disputes are settled by negotiation between the management and the union, or if this breaks down, a decision is made by arbitration by an outside third party, which is binding on both sides.

In some cases contracts stipulate 'closed shop' arrangements, by which management may employ only members of the union concerned. More common is the 'union shop,' by which employees are required to join the union after being employed. In the 'agency shop,' employees are required to pay union dues whether or not they are members.

Of course, many workers do not belong to a union and are not covered by a contract. To protect them, there is legislation setting out minimum employment standards. It covers wages, hours of work, overtime arrangements, statutory holidays, vacations, and such matters. Separate boards oversee safety arrangements in the various industries.

TRANSPORT

Even worse than the Rockies, the rugged country north and north-east of Lake Superior is a formidable barrier between Eastern Canada and the west. It has posed enormous problems for those engineering transport routes, and for those trying to operate them.

The area contains thousands of lakes and the dense rock of the Shield. In the 1880s it drove the builders of the Canadian Pacific Railway to despair and nearly to bankruptcy. But their line showed its usefulness just in time, as it transported troops from the east to face the 1885 Riel rising on the Prairies.

The railway went through and superseded the old canoe portage routes. The line prospered in spite of the vast distances it had to cover, and in the years before World War I, two new transcontinental railways were built to compete with it. However, they were not viable and in 1917 combined with lesser lines to become the Canadian National Railway.

In Southern Ontario there was, by this time, a flourishing network of lines joining the many communities, including those formerly of the Grand Trunk Railway, which is now part of the Canadian National Railway. Besides, in 1900 the Ontario government had commissioned a new line heading north from the CPR station at North Bay.

This was the construction project which brought about the discovery of Cobalt and, subsequently, the northern goldfields. The line was built in stages, and by 1932 reached Moosonee on James Bay. Today the Ontario Northland links several mining and pulpmill towns along its route, but it is most famous for its Polar Bear Express to Moosonee.

The development of roads in Ontario predated railway building by many decades, but early efforts were not impressive. Simcoe's military roads long remained the basis of land transportation, and to them was added a system of 'colonization' roads — bush tracks not infrequently punctuated by sawn-off stumps each a metre high.

After 1825 several private companies undertook to improve matters by building toll roads or turnpikes, maintained at travellers' expense. Then, in 1835, a plank road was constructed near Toronto — the first of many. From 1837 on, they were slowly replaced by roads made of macadamized bitumen or tar laid over gravel and larger stones.

Today, the King's Highway is the responsibility of the provincial government, while municipalities and regional authorities build and maintain lesser roads. Important highways include the Macdonald-Cartier Freeway (Highway 401), from the American border crossing at Windsor to the Quebec boundary, which in some urban centres is twelve lanes wide.

Other highways are the Queen Elizabeth Way from Toronto to Niagara, which includes the impressive Burlington Skyway; Highway 400, from Toronto north to Barrie; and in the north, the Ontario section of the Trans-Canada Highway, which runs from the Ottawa valley to the Manitoba boundary via Thunder Bay. Like the railways, it met construction problems north of Lake Superior.

A third form of surface transportation is the pipeline, used to convey liquids and gases. Natural gas from Western Canada is pumped to Toronto and then Montreal by way of Thunder Bay, Kapuskasing, and North Bay. Crude oil from the west reaches refineries at Sarnia via a pipeline crossing Minnesota from Manitoba.

There are several deep-water harbours in the province, each run by a commission responsible to the federal Department of Transport. They include Toronto, Hamilton, Windsor, Oshawa, Lakehead (Thunder Bay), and Belleville. Another harbour is Moosonee on James Bay, but it is open only three months of the year so it is not heavily utilized.

Ontario has two international airports — at Malton, near Toronto, and at Ottawa. Both are the responsibility of the federal government. Otherwise there are many municipal airports, and the

Metropolitan Toronto contains many complex highway intersections, designed to expedite traffic flow and minimize accidents. Here the 401 — properly known as the Macdonald-Cartier Freeway, which runs from Windsor to the Quebec boundary — intersects the Spadina Expressway.

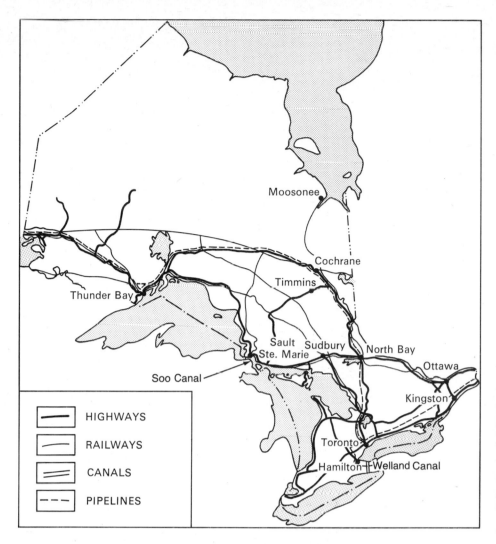

province has constructed a grid of all-weather strips in Northern Ontario to serve general aviation all year round.

Recent years have seen great advances in urban transportation systems, hopefully an antidote to the rising number of automobiles. Metropolitan Toronto has a fully integrated transport system, including subways, buses, and streetcars. In addition, the province runs the GO transit system, linking the Toronto area with surrounding municipalities.

Map legend:
- HIGHWAYS
- RAILWAYS
- CANALS
- PIPELINES

The pride of the passenger rail service between Toronto and Montreal is the distinctive Turbo, which covers the distance at an average speed of 135 km/h. Canadian National operates five trains to provide the service, each consisting of seven cars.

Light aircraft are in many cases lifelines of northern communities. Traditionally float planes have been used, taking advantage of the tens of thousands of lakes in Northern Ontario. For winter conditions the planes have been equipped with skis, but in recent years the provincial government has developed a network of all-weather landing strips throughout the north, to be used in all seasons.

Container transport means that goods need only minimal handling between source and destination, whether carried by road, rail, or water. This is a scene at Toronto's container terminal.

THE SEAWAY

The deep waterway from Montreal to Lake Superior links the heart of North America with the Atlantic and the world beyond. It is one of the world's busiest shipping routes and ranks in significance with the Panama and Suez Canals.

The idea of a deep draft waterway to open up the Great Lakes was first proposed in the 1890s. Before World War I, Canada developed a canal system to bypass the various rapids on the St. Lawrence, but its locks were less than 5 m deep. In the 1930s the old Welland Canal at Niagara was rebuilt to take bigger ships.

But for a Seaway, more elaborate arrangements were needed. Canada and the United States discussed possibilities but could not agree. Then, in 1951, Canada announced that it was ready to proceed alone, though for a quite different purpose. Both Ontario and New York State were in urgent need of more power from the St. Lawrence river.

With that the Americans came to terms. It was agreed that Ontario and New York State should build the necessary generating and control dams, and that the governments of Canada and the United States should deepen the waterway and, where necessary, adapt and build locks in their respective sectors.

The Seaway opened in 1959. Canada's contribution had been to dredge the lower reaches of the St. Lawrence and to extend four locks above Montreal, to build a lock around the control dam at Iroquois, and to modify the eight locks in the Welland system. The Americans built two major locks around the generating dam near Cornwall.

From the Atlantic to the far west of Lake Superior, the Seaway extends nearly 3800 km. Ships going all the way must negotiate seven locks in the St. Lawrence section, eight more in the Welland section, and at Sault Ste. Marie they use one of four parallel locks on the American side, or a smaller system in Canada.

The locks on the St. Lawrence and Welland systems — the Seaway proper — are designed to standard dimensions: usable length 233.5 m, usable width 24.4 m, and depth over sills 9.1 m. This has encouraged the building of special 'laker' ships, particularly the

The famous flight locks on the Welland Canal offer two-way traffic for vessels on their way up or down the Seaway.

Thunder Bay on Lake Superior has long been an important transshipping point for wheat from the western provinces. These are the elevators in which the wheat awaits shipment to ports on the St. Lawrence, from where it is exported.

730s (for 730 ft length) designed to fit snugly in the locks.

The 730s are bulk carriers intended to carry the staple cargoes of the Seaway — iron ore from Quebec and Labrador to Hamilton or one of the American steel towns on Lake Erie; and grain from Canada's west, shipped from Thunder Bay to Quebec's Atlantic ports. There the grain is transshipped for an ocean crossing.

Lakers can carry some 27 000 tonnes of iron ore, or more than 36 000 m³ of wheat. The ships are long and narrow, with the machinery astern and the navigating bridge forward. In locks and canals they are carefully monitored on electronic equipment, which oversees every operation.

The Seaway also carries great quantities of general cargo to and from the many industrial ports it serves. Most ocean-going ships carry about 10 000 tonnes, though some are much bigger. In recent years there has been great expansion in containerized cargoes, and much grain, coal, and fuel oil is carried in bulk.

More than a dozen ports in Ontario are served by the Seaway, but those principally affected are Hamilton and Toronto, as industrial centres, and Thunder Bay at the lakehead. Others include Windsor and Oshawa, Sault Ste. Marie (particularly for steel), Sarnia (for petroleum products), St. Catharines, and Port Colborne.

One serious limitation of the Seaway is that in winter it is ice-bound, and for four months navigation is impossible. Icebreakers of the Canadian Coast Guard keep shipping channels open as long as possible before the Seaway closes for the winter, both in the lakes region and on the St. Lawrence.

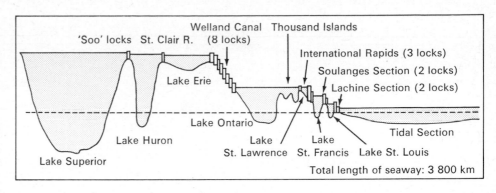

The lock systems for Sault Ste. Marie, the Welland Canal, and the St. Lawrence compensate for differences in water level between the Great Lakes and the sea.

Special '730' bulk carriers ply the Seaway, designed to take maximum advantage of the proportions of the locks en route. Staple cargoes for the lakers are wheat and iron ore.

The locks of Sault Ste. Marie, between Lakes Huron and Superior, are a popular tourist attraction.

NUCLEAR POWER

A major factor in Ontario's continued prosperity has been an abundance of cheap energy. In earlier days nearly all of it was hydroelectricity — water power harnessed at Niagara Falls, from the Ottawa river, and in scores of less spectacular locations.

As energy needs increased and all major sources of water power were utilized, the province's Hydro authority turned increasingly to steam power — thermal energy produced by burning fossil fuels like coal, natural gas, and oil. Like falling water, steam is used to drive giant turbines, which in turn generate electricity.

However, fossil fuels are non-renewable resources and are best reserved for more important functions than merely to produce steam heat. Besides, Ontario is obliged to import them — oil and gas from the western provinces and outside Canada, and coal from the west and the United States. The high cost both of materials and transportation defeats the aim of providing cheap energy.

Instead, the province has shown increasing interest in the one fuel resource of which it has abundant supply — natural uranium. In the years following World War II, first the National Research Council and then Atomic Energy of Canada developed the technology now used in the CANDU nuclear reactor.

CANDU stands for Canada Deuterium Uranium, the deuterium being elements of 'heavy water' introduced to slow down a spontaneous chain reaction in the natural uranium. Certain atoms in the uranium are continually in motion, exchanging neutrons which normally travel so fast that they penetrate surrounding matter as a ray.

However, when these neutrons are slowed down — as they are when they bounce off large hydrogen atoms in the heavy water — they hit other atoms rather than pass through them, and cause one type in particular to split. This split is called 'fission,' which in turn triggers more neutrons and produces heat. In the CANDU system, this interaction generates steam.

If allowed to run out of control, the chain reaction could produce dangerously high levels of power and heat in

The Bruce nuclear power complex is near Port Elgin on Lake Huron. It includes generating facilities and plants manufacturing heavy water for use in the reactors.

Ontario Hydro relies on hydroelectric power for the bulk of its requirements, drawing it from such stations as Des Joachims on the Ottawa river. The station has been in service since 1950. ▼

the reactor. But with careful supervision, there is minimal chance that this will happen. Pellets of uranium are contained in non-corrosive zircaloy rods, which are literally bundled into the reactor.

Basically the reactor is a cylindrical tank filled with heavy water, through which pass tubes containing the bundles of rods and a second, separate system of pipes containing heavy water to transfer heat. To contain radioactivity — the passage of rays, which can cause cancer by upsetting the chemical balance in living matter — the reactor is heavily shielded in thick concrete.

In a typical reactor, each bundle survives for up to eighteen months, until its original power has faded to the point where it should be replaced. However it remains active, so it must be stored in such a way that its rays can do no harm. It now contains a new element as a by-product of the fission process — plutonium.

It is the plutonium which causes the greatest difficulty, for it is still so lively that it can itself by utilized as an energy source. In fact, Ontario nuclear power stations store waste fuels in anticipation of a time when it is economic to recover the plutonium and use it in adapted CANDU reactors.

For the present, however, the wastes are stored deep under water, which slows down and absorbs any neutrons that escape. Ultimately the wastes will be stored underground in locations where radioactive materials cannot reach the natural water table — perhaps in saltbeds or deep in the solid rock of the Shield.

So far, Ontario has two major nuclear power projects in operation. The Pickering station, 28 km east of Toronto, opened in 1971 and has four reactors. The Bruce complex, on Lake Huron, is one of the world's largest and is accompanied by a trio of chemical plants making heavy water. Ontario Hydro has plans to establish several others.

Already thermal power, as opposed to water generation, accounts for 60 per cent of Ontario's electricity requirements, and the proportion will necessarily increase. Much of it will be borne by the expanding nuclear facilities, but much of it will be carried by stations burning fossil fuels, which can adjust their output as required.

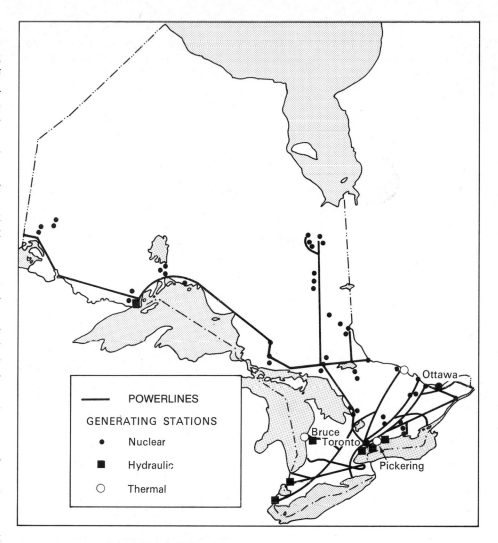

POWERLINES

GENERATING STATIONS

• Nuclear

■ Hydraulic

○ Thermal

Ottawa

Bruce
Toronto

Pickering

Zirconium tubes containing natural uranium are bundled, then loaded into one of the four reactors at the Bruce nuclear power station.

Ontario Hydro's electric power grid connects sources with consumers and is linked with neighbouring systems in Quebec, Manitoba, and the United States.

Power stations burning fossil fuels like coal and oil provide extra power at times of peak demand. This is the Lambton coal-burning station south of Sarnia.

COMMUNITIES

In its origins Ontario depended chiefly on agriculture, and its first settled communities were local centres of trade and distribution. They included Toronto, Kingston, London, Peterborough, Guelph, Cornwall, Cobourg, Kitchener, and Waterloo.

Other communities came to prominence with the development of trade routes. Sault Ste. Marie dominated the passage from Lake Huron to Lake Superior. St. Catharines profited from the completion of the first Welland Canal in 1829. Ottawa, or rather Bytown, was originally the headquarters camp for construction of the Rideau Canal.

Then came the railways. Hamilton and Windsor became important depots for the Great Western, and the railway workshops established in these and other localities encouraged the growth of local industries. North Bay was selected as a key depot for the Canadian Pacific and was the junction for the Ontario government's line to the north.

That project led to the discovery of the rich mineral deposits in the area, and to new communities like Timmins and Kirkland Lake. The Canadian Pacific had already given rise to Sudbury farther west and strengthened the position of Sault Ste. Marie, which could now be reached throughout the winter, whereas before it had been marooned.

With the activities of the Canadian Pacific in the 1880s, there was new prosperity for Fort William, long since eclipsed as a key link in the fur trade. Later the railways made neighbouring Port Arthur their terminal for grain from the prairies, though in 1970 its identity and Fort William's were merged in the new City of Thunder Bay.

Improved transport brought new opportunities to exploit the resources of remote areas. New communities sprang up in support of a single industry — whether mining, as in Elliot Lake and Atikokan, or pulp and paper, as in Kenora, Dryden, and Kapuskasing. Soon service industry was introduced to support major enterprise and trade as well.

In the south, however, the emphasis was on manufacturing. Toronto and Hamilton were best placed to take advantage of Canadian markets, and these two developed fastest. But their new zest

Kingston, near the eastern end of Lake Ontario, is one of Ontario's prettiest cities. It was established by Loyalists in 1783 on the site of Frontenac's Fort Cataraqui, which was erected in 1673. Kingston is the most significant community in Eastern Ontario, apart from Ottawa, the national capital.

Kenora is the western-most community in Ontario, situated on Lake of the Woods near the Manitoba boundary. It is significant as a centre of the pulp and paper industry.

was reflected all around the Golden Horseshoe, from Oshawa to Niagara-on-the-Lake, and, indeed, all through south-western Ontario.

In recent years communities in Central Ontario have profited from the leisure boom closely related to the prosperity of the south, particularly those in the picturesque regions adjoining Georgian Bay. Farther north, communities once remote have flourished through the patronage of outdoors enthusiasts, including hunters and fishermen.

As a province, Ontario has encouraged the incorporation of communities as municipalities, upon which they are delegated powers of self-government. These communities may be villages, towns, or cities, depending on their population and the recognition of the Ontario Municipal Board.

Since 1968 the provincial government has encouraged a system of two-tier government, by which neighbouring municipalities federate and delegate members to sit on a regional council. This is made responsible for certain broad areas of control, while individual municipalities continue to run purely local services.

A typical division of duties makes the regional authority responsible for police, fire-fighting, and ambulance services throughout the area, as well as a public transport system, water purification, garbage and sewage disposal, and main roads. The local authority might regulate water mains, garbage collection, subsidiary roads, and so on.

Not the least advantage of the regional system is that it provides a more even spread of tax responsibility. Local authorities draw most of their revenue from property taxation, so must calculate a suitable 'mill rate' by which to multiply an assessment factor on all industrial, business, and residential premises throughout the district.

More than two-thirds of Ontario's population is governed by these two-tier local authorities. Further expansion of the scheme is unlikely, since rural communities are not easily co-ordinated. Instead, the province has supported the rise of county councils, which incorporate existing municipalities with the rural community around them.

Ottawa

With Quebec across the river, residents of Ottawa are very much aware that they live in Ontario. They elect representatives to the provincial parliament in Toronto; they are subject to Ontario laws and pay Ontario taxes; their children are schooled in terms of the Ontario education system; their cars carry Ontario registration.

However, Ontarians elsewhere in the province seldom remember that Ottawa is part of it. They tend to consider the National Capital Region (Ottawa and Hull) as an entity in itself, as if it were a federal responsibility.

The view might appear fair, as Ottawa's character is in stark contrast with those cities elsewhere in Ontario, apart from Toronto. The national capital's population is drawn from all regions of Canada and (if one counts the diplomatic corps) from all over the world.

In spite of this, Ottawa holds a large number of true Ontarian families, who are proud to belong to the province. The provincial government and Ottawa's own municipality play major roles in developing the community. In any case, the surrounding countryside holds a distinctively Ontarian population, in no way affected by the cosmopolitan excitement of the capital.

A view of Ottawa's Parliament Buildings and the National Arts Centre. In the foreground is the Rideau Canal, on which construction started in 1827. 'Bytown,' the construction headquarters on its banks, was selected as capital of the Canadas and was renamed Ottawa in 1860.

The oldest community in Ontario is Moose Factory, situated on an island in the Moose river, upstream of James Bay and established in 1730 by the Hudson's Bay Company. The island lies opposite present-day Moosonee (shown here), the northern terminus of the Ontario Northland Railway and potentially a significant port outlet on James Bay.

Population

According to the Statistics Canada mini-census of 1976, Metropolitan Toronto is Canada's largest metropolitan area, with a population of 2 803 101, just ahead of Montreal at 2 802 845. The mini-census listed several Ontario metropolitan areas with large populations. Among them are the following:

Hamilton	529 371
Ottawa	521 341
St. Catharines-Niagara	301 921
Kitchener	272 158
London	270 383
Windsor	247 582

MONEY MARKETS

Pre-eminent among Ontario's communities is the City of Toronto — or rather Metropolitan Toronto, the federation of the city and the five surrounding boroughs, which are effectively its suburbs.

Metropolitan Toronto dominates Canada's industrial production — not least because so much of the consumer market is close by. As a result, Toronto's downtown area is Canada's financial heavyweight. The business district is squeezed between Yonge Street and University Avenue, centred on Bay Street and the Toronto Stock Exchange.

The concept of a stock exchange is that companies needing capital may raise it by selling shares to the public. These shares will hopefully earn dividends from the companies' profits and are valuable in themselves. The exchange is a market place for the buying and selling of their shares.

The Toronto exchange is one of the world's busiest, and in the Americas it is second only to New York's. It was formed in 1934 on the amalgamation of two rival exchanges and consists of 126 'seats.' The seats may be held by corporations, partnerships, or sole proprietorships, though no one firm or proprietor may hold more than three.

Each seat held entitles the firm concerned to depute up to five representatives to trade on the exchange floor. The firm's phone clerk informs them which shares are to be bought or sold on the orders of clients, and they seek out representatives of other firms with whom they negotiate a price. This is agreed verbally, then recorded.

Members of the stock exchange and other firms dealing in securities are known as 'investment dealers.' These securities are usually either stocks and shares (of several types) or bonds (by which municipalities, corporations, and other bodies raise money).

Closely concerned with securities and the capital market in general are Canada's chartered banks, and particularly the 'big five,' which control some 90 per cent of their total assets. Three of these — the Canadian Imperial Bank of Commerce, the Toronto Dominion Bank, and the Bank of Nova Scotia — have their headquarters in downtown Toronto.

Toronto's commercial centre is the heart of the downtown area, its highrise office blocks within easy reach of their neighbours. Not far away is the CN Tower, which doubles as a communications centre and as a tourist attraction, complete with viewing galleries and restaurant. It is the world's tallest free-standing structure.

Under the Canadian system, a chartered bank accepts savings deposits and makes loans, whether personal or commercial. It conducts most of its business through branches spread throughout the country. Each branch is equipped to provide almost every service to do with money, its safeguarding, transfer, and conversion.

Each chartered bank is a corporation owned outright by its shareholders, and bank shares are bought on stock exchanges like any other shares. As with most corporations, the shareholders elect a board of directors to dictate general policy on their behalf, and the directors entrust day-to-day implementation to a chief executive officer.

By law only the chartered banks — the federal Bank of Canada and its subsidiary, the Industrial Development Bank, and the Montreal City and District Savings Bank — are entitled to refer to themselves as 'banks.' However, there are other financial institutions entitled to carry out particular functions of the banking process.

One group is 'trust companies,' some of which operate country-wide branches like the chartered banks. Originally their prime concern was administration of property and investments. They concentrated on making orderly arrangements for the best use of personal and business assets, particularly in regard to on-going administration in the event of death. But in recent years they have undertaken many functions formerly closed to them by law. In particular, they now accept high interest savings accounts.

Money may be borrowed through banks and trust companies on the strength of the inherent value of real property, often residential, or through finance companies on the security of 'chattels' purchased (perhaps furniture, a car, or a colour television). In each case — as with any loan — appropriate interest must be paid by the borrower.

The 'life insurance company,' in contrast, offers financial security in the event of death, cash settlement on retirement, and pension plans. Closely related is disability coverage, while general insurance is available on practically any commodity or situation, provided acceptable premiums and conditions can be worked out.

The Toronto Stock Exchange is one of the world's busiest. It was founded in 1934 on the amalgamation of two rival exchanges.

Computerized services play a major role in modern commercial banking and throughout the financial world. ▼

Also of note are provincial savings branches administered by Ontario's Department of Revenue, and a league of provincially chartered credit unions, which operate like banks except that they may serve only their members and not the public at large. They are in a position to accept savings and advance loans, and to pay annual dividends on each share.

TORONTO

As the focal point of the middle third of Canada's consumer market, Toronto is well endowed with shops, department stores, and supermarkets. The most fashionable shopping district is the Yorkville area and the Bloor–Yonge intersection, but most money is spent in the suburbs.

In fact, Toronto's suburbs have pioneered the shopping style which seems ideally suited to Canada's climate — the indoor, all-in-one, pedestrian mall planned to serve all the shopping (and in many cases recreational) needs of the surrounding community. Malls are well patronized on weekends and when they stay open after regular business hours.

Somehow a well-designed mall is far more glamorous than a street of stores, and the lesson has not been wasted on downtown planners. Each year new malls come into operation in the business district, and modern office de-

The time may come when it is possible to walk throughout downtown Toronto underground. Already a number of underground shopping malls and walkways link office blocks. A major advance came with the opening of the Eaton Centre in 1977, shown here, the world's biggest store complex.

Toronto has a number of international restaurants — among them the world's highest, on top of the CN Tower and overlooking the highrise blocks of the city centre.

velopments expect to incorporate an underground shopping mall, if possible linked to the subway system.

The most exciting flowering of the new idea has been the Eaton Centre opened in 1977, which is probably the most advanced mall in North America. Quite possibly shoppers of the future will be able to walk throughout downtown Toronto without once having to emerge into the cold outside — an important consideration for six months of the year.

The upgrading of facilities is an important factor in keeping a city's heart alive. Fortunately Toronto has no problems on that score, since in the 1970s it has emerged as one of the liveliest in North America. Theatres, cinemas, discos, restaurants, clubs, and bars are thriving.

One of the brightest features is the proliferation of live music. Classical, jazz, folk, and rock have enthusiastic followings. An immense variety is offered, including many free concerts in downtown churches and public squares. There are celebrity concerts almost daily in Toronto's many theatres and auditoriums, and outdoors in summer.

Besides music, a great variety of alternative cultural activity is offered throughout the year. Neighbourhood libraries act as temples of the arts, featuring films, discussions, and classes. Toronto's Harbourfront has a free nightly program of films, poetry, theatre, or music, including square dancing and jazz.

Then there are the institutions. The city has a score of museums, including the Royal Ontario Museum, which is Canada's largest and which incorporates the McLaughlin Planetarium. The museum specializes in the structure of the earth, its animals (past and present), and

The Ontario Science Centre in Don Mills was opened in 1967 as Ontario's celebration of a century of Confederation. Its scientific and technological displays encourage visitor participation as many can be touched and activated, and the centre combines the features of museum, school, university, and exhibition.

Of various art collections the most important are at the Art Gallery of Ontario, re-opened in 1974 after extensive reconstruction. The gallery's special pride is its Henry Moore sculpture collection, donated by the artist. In 1977 it opened a special wing to display its fine collection of Canadian art.

Ontario Place is a complex of attractions on a clutch of man-made islands on the waterfront — Toronto's answer to Montreal's Expo. Its Forum is an open-air amphitheatre which stages everything from symphony concerts to native dancing, but the best patronized item is the Children's Village, complete with fascinating audio-visual displays.

Each year Toronto stages the Canadian National Exhibition, the world's longest-running annual fair of its size. It combines trade, agriculture, sport, music, and a huge midway. But in international prestige it is overshadowed by the Royal Agricultural Winter Fair, which features several world championship contests.

its civilizations, from Babylon to early Canada.

Toronto has several 'living museums.' One is Fort York, which was abandoned in the War of 1812, but which has since been restored. Black Creek Pioneer Village, in Downsview, illustrates life in Upper Canada before 1867. Casa Loma is like a medieval castle, a rich man's folly, complete with great hall and secret passages. It was built between 1911 and 1914.

Each fall Toronto hosts the Canadian National Exhibition, the longest-running annual fair of its significance. The exhibition is an agricultural and trade fair, a cultural festival, and an amusement park combined.

In North America only New York's Broadway tops Toronto theatre, which offers productions to suit every taste. Theatres are well supported, both by Torontonians and by visitors to Toronto.

CULTURAL MOSAIC

For nine days each summer Toronto goes *en fête* with its International Caravan, a celebration of the city's ethnic diversity. Greeks, Japanese, Ukrainians, and scores of other groups operate pavilions named after cities of the world.

Since its modest foundation in 1969, Caravan has grown into a major festival, attracting tens of thousands of visitors. The pavilions are scattered throughout Toronto, and where possible, in the heart of the neighbourhoods that have organized them. Visitors are equipped with 'passports,' which entitle them to enter each and sample its attractions.

These include food, wine, and entertainment typical of the city involved — which might be Berlin or Belgrade, Seoul or Seville. A typical evening might take the visitor to Hungary, Hong Kong, Trinidad, and Israel. Each pavilion is as authentic as its organizers can make it, and caters both to the inquisitive and the homesick.

Of course much of what the festival highlights is permanently present in

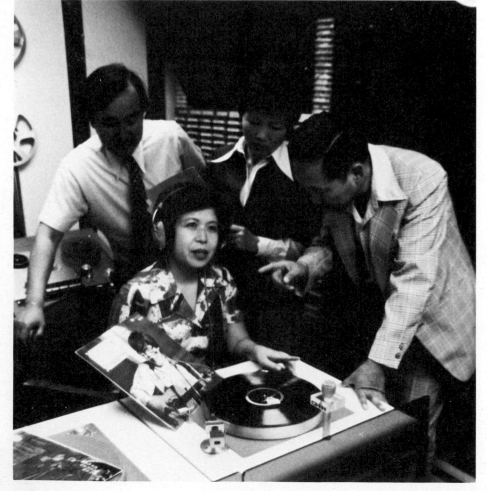

Korean Canadians discuss program content at CHIN, Toronto's multicultural radio station. CHIN broadcasts in more than thirty languages to ethnic audiences in southwestern Ontario, among them Italian, German, Portuguese, Dutch, Polish, Ukrainian, Greek, and Chinese.

Mennonites, a Christian sect of German origin, live a deliberately simple rural existence and spurn manufactured commodities in favour of goods they can produce through their own efforts. A large group is settled in the Kitchener-Waterloo region.

Toronto. The city blooms with exotic cuisine — French, Spanish, Hungarian, Greek, Italian, Chinese, and many other varieties. Nearly eighty different languages are spoken regularly — and English is spoken by arrivals from five continents.

The new Canadians have greatly changed the face of Toronto, which outsiders used to revile as dull and puritanical. The newcomers have given it new zest — a taste for active outdoor living imported from faraway countries with many months of hot sunshine. In addition they have contributed a new cultural depth, particularly in the arts.

Painters and sculptors have come from Europe and Asia, playwrights and poets from the United States, and musicians from all over the world. Indeed, music is the field in which Toronto has gained most — whether orchestral or chamber, or in the Canadian Opera Company, which came into being on the encouragement of new Canadians.

Many of the immigrants adapt swiftly to their new environment. Others are not so fortunate. It is they who excite special concern in government circles, which have been made aware of sometimes enormous cultural differ-

ences separating new arrivals from their Canadian neighbours and from each other.

One area of special difficulty is education. A public school class might include children from the West Indies, Pakistan, Italy, Yugoslavia, and Scotland. Yet the teacher is probably Canadian, struggling not simply with difficulties of language and accent, but also with wholly different backgrounds and assumptions.

Conversely, contrasting attitudes may be expressed in the students' homes. An Italian girl may be forbidden by her parents to take part in social activities. An East Indian boy familiar with Canadian freedom of decision may resent his parents' insistence that they arrange his marriage for him.

Similar problems arise wherever there are customs to be misunderstood. A Portuguese might suppose that hospital is a last resort, and that a relative referred there must be at death's door. A patrolling policeman might not realize that young men gathered on a street corner are there to socialize, as in Mediterranean lands or the West Indies, and not to plan mischief.

One mistake commonly made is to suppose that the Canadian mosaic involves only immigrants. Instead, it concerns all sectors of the population. Even established Ontarian society is varied, involving those of English, Scottish,

Kitchener was originally named Berlin but was 'patriotically' renamed during World War I. An annual Oktoberfest is organized to recall the region's strong German heritage.

Ontario attracts immigrants from all over the world, and a high proportion of them settle in Toronto. Certain neighbourhoods have a distinct ethnic flavour — for instance, Italian or Ukrainian — but many cultures contribute to the diversity of the Kensington market.

Irish, and American heritage, as well as Franco–Ontarians (especially in the east and north) and native Indians.

Then there are exclusive groups which have managed to preserve their own identity through generations. The prime example is the Mennonite community of Kitchener (which was known as Berlin until the name was changed in World War I). The original German settlers arrived in Upper Canada in 1807 by way of Pennsylvania.

Ontario's Ukrainians have taken more pains than most to keep their culture alive, because in its native home it has been muzzled and has nearly perished. Blacks have lived in Upper Canada since the earliest settlement, and some are descended from those who had hair-raising adventures escaping slavery in the United States' south.

For all these cultures, newly arrived or long-established, Ontario lays down one Human Rights Code. This prohibits discrimination on the grounds of race, creed, colour, sex, marital status, ancestry, nationality, place of origin, or age, whether in employment, in access to services or facilities available to the public, or in related advertising.

At the start of a session of the Ontario legislature, the province's lieutenant-governor reads the 'speech from the throne.' The lieutenant-governor represents the monarch and outlines the legislative program planned by the government.

QUEEN'S PARK

Besides the ninety-odd members they elect to Canada's House of Commons in Ottawa, Ontarians send 117 representatives to their provincial parliament in Toronto. These MPPs reach Queen's Park through elections held at least once every five years.

In many countries, provincial assemblies are subservient to their national government and have relatively minor powers. But in Canada the provinces enjoy considerable authority, and the provincial parliamentarian is responsible for more areas of public concern than his federal counterpart.

These areas include health and education, local government, property and civil rights — which the courts have decided include labour legislation and social security — administration of justice, incorporation of provincial companies, and powers of direct taxation. With few reservations the province can change its own constitution.

But what gives a provincial government special power is that it administers Crown property for the public good. In absolute terms, the whole province (possibly excepting Indian lands) is Crown property. In practice, responsibility is for 'unalienated' Crown land (land not sold or leased) including waterways, and natural resources including minerals, forests, and wildlife.

In the assembly the MPPs comment on and criticize the policies suggested by the provincial cabinet to cover these fields, and hopefully ensure that they reflect the wishes of the population. Besides this they review the expenditure of government departments in implementing the policies, a safeguard which is the basis of responsible government.

The MPPs assemble at Queen's Park at least once a year. Queen's Park is the property of the University of Toronto, but was leased to the City of Toronto in 1850 for 999 years providing that a site

was reserved for the provincial government. However, until 1866 the site of the present buildings was occupied by a lunatic asylum.

Following Confederation the provincial government met in premises on Front Street, but in 1880 it voted funds for a new building. An international architectural competition was held to select a design, but the chairman of the judges — R. A. Waite, an Englishman living in Buffalo — claimed he could do a better job and was commissioned.

Waite's eventual design was for a building which seemed enormous for the needs of the day, and which eventually cost nearly three times the amount originally budgeted. The bulk of it was built of brownstone from quarries near Orangeville, and deep blue slates for the roof came from Vermont. Waite was lavish with copper and cast iron.

The result was described by contemporaries as 'far from beautiful by modern standards, but rather monolithic in its domination of the head of the avenue.' And that is the impression it still conveys. It was opened with great pomp in April 1893, and a fashionable crowd gathered to observe the legislators in their new home.

Its centrepiece is the assembly chamber, panelled in mahogany and Canadian sycamore and surmounted by wood carvings. At one end is Mr. Speaker's chair. Mr. Speaker is elected by the MPPs at the beginning of the first session of each parliament to act as their spokesman and preside over their deliberations.

At the head of Toronto's University Avenue are the legislative buildings opened in 1893. These house Ontario's parliament.

Recent Ontario elections have been contested by three well-balanced parties — the Progressive Conservatives, the Liberals, and the New Democrats (NDP). The Progressive Conservatives — known in Ontario as 'the big blue machine' — have held power since 1943.

On Mr. Speaker's right are the benches occupied by the government, normally drawn from the party with the most members elected, and consisting of the premier (usually its leader) and the cabinet he has selected. Each minister has sworn loyalty to the Crown and is normally responsible for one or more departments of the public service.

Her Majesty's Loyal Opposition sits on Mr. Speaker's left, and normally consists of members of parties defeated in the election. The biggest of these parties is the official opposition,

and it provides the leader of the opposition who co-ordinates the various challenges to government policy and operations.

Elsewhere in the building is the suite of the province's lieutenant-governor, who represents the Queen. A provincial government proper consists of the 'lieutenant-governor-in-council,' the council being the cabinet. Even when passed by the MPPs, no bill can become law until it bears the lieutenant-governor's signature.

Near the parliament buildings are

various blocks of offices which accommodate many of Ontario's public servants. They are named after former provincial premiers — Macdonald, Mowat, Whitney, Hearst, Ferguson, Hepburn, Drew, and Frost. Macdonald was not John A., but his near namesake, John Sandfield.

The Policy and Priorities Board is the nerve centre of Ontario's provincial government. It meets regularly to discuss action proposed in the various policy fields and makes recommendations to the cabinet.

RESOURCES
DEVELOPMENT FIELD
Agriculture & Food
Energy
Environment
Industry & Tourism
Labour
Natural Resources
Northern Affairs
Transportation &
Communications

OFFICE OF THE
PREMIER
CABINET OFFICE

SOCIAL
DEVELOPMENT
POLICY FIELD
Colleges & Universities
Community & Social Services
Education
Health
Northern Affairs

POLICY &
PRIORITIES BOARD
Premier, Treasurer
Provincial Secretaries
Minister of Energy
Chairman of
Management Board

Management
Board of Cabinet
Government Services
Civil Service Commission

JUSTICE
POLICY FIELD
Attorney General
Consumer &
Commercial Relations
Correctional Services
Northern Affairs

TREASURY,
ECONOMICS AND
INTERGOVERNMENTAL
AFFAIRS
REVENUE
HOUSING

GOVERNMENT

Before 1972, Ontario's government was characterized by a series of vertical departments, most with rigidly defined responsibilities. Each was headed by a minister sitting in the cabinet, but there was little formal co-ordination of program and policy planning.

Inevitably distinctions blurred and there were conflicts of interest. In 1969 the lieutenant-governor-in-council appointed a 'committee into government productivity' to recommend fresh procedures. Half its members were senior public servants; the other half were senior executives from the business world.

The committee undertook a major study of the ojectives of government both in Canada and in other countries. Eventually it produced a master plan designed to co-ordinate the activities of the many departments, obliging them to work together. Most of the recommendations were implemented in a major government reorganization in 1972.

The chief emphasis of the new plan was on consistent policy. Individual ministries were to frame policy alternatives. These were to be evaluated and balanced by 'policy field committees' covering related ministries. The committees' recommendations were to be incorporated as government policy by a 'policy and priorities board.'

The final step was the approval of the cabinet and formal instruction to the cabinet's management board to have the program initiated by the appropriate ministry or by some other government agency. By this system all other government departments would be aware of the new provision and could adjust their programs accordingly.

The effect of the reorganization was to concentrate government activity in three chief policy fields — resource development, social development, and justice, reflecting the major areas of responsibility entrusted to the province by the British North America Act of 1867 and subsequent court decisions. The Ministry of Northern Affairs created in 1977 was designed to cover all three fields in Northern Ontario.

'Resources development' covers activities of the Ministries of Agriculture and Food, Energy, Environment, Housing, Industry and Tourism, Labour, Natural Resources, Northern Affairs, and Transportation and Communications. 'Social development' accounts for the Ministries of Colleges and Universities, Education, Health, and Community and Social Services.

'Justice' embraces the Ministries of the Attorney-General, Consumer and Commercial Relations, Correctional Services, and the Solicitor-General. A fourth group of ministries covers administrative, financial, and economic matters, relations with other governments, and planning — Government Services, Revenue, and Treasury Economics and Intergovernmental Affairs.

In many ways the last-named ministry — TEIGA for short — is the most powerful of all. Besides being responsible for the provincial budget, it is the chief arbiter on overall economic policy within the province and also on development in particular regions.

Interestingly, TEIGA also handles Ontario's dealings not only with the federal government and sister provincial governments (particularly Quebec's), but also with all local authorities. This means that TEIGA liaises with all levels of government, from highest to lowest, and at the same time with all spheres of government across the province.

Local government is the responsibility of the province, but in practice it is delegated to municipalities. These include regional governments, which are upper houses responsible for planning, and other regional services in a group of neighbouring municipalities. Individual municipalities attend to basic day-to-day services in their respective areas.

The province has extensive powers of direct taxation, but delegates some (property taxation and business licensing) to local authorities. Other major sources of income are personal income tax (collected by the federal government on Ontario's behalf), retail sales tax, corporation tax, and gasoline and motor vehicle fuel tax.

The Premiers

There have been few major upsets in Ontario's political history since Confederation, though in 1919 the United Farmers (UF) of Ontario swept the Conservatives (C) out of office by promising major economies. They came to grief when the Conservatives claimed that the premier, E. C. Drury, had installed in his office a brass coal-scuttle worth $100.

The Liberals (L) came into power in 1934 under Mitchell Hepburn, an onion farmer also pledged to cut government spending. His administration was characterized by mass dismissal of civil servants hired by the Conservatives, and the public auctioning of Ontario's forty-seven official cars. But the Conservatives — restyled 'Progressive Conservatives' (PC) in 1942 — returned to power in 1943.

Here is a list of Ontario's premiers since Confederation:

John Sandfield Macdonald (Coalition)	1867–1871
Edward Blake (L)	1871–1872
Oliver Mowat (L)	1872–1896
A. S. Hardy (L)	1896–1899
George Ross (L)	1899–1905
John Whitney (C)	1905–1914
William Hearst (C)	1914–1919
Ernest Drury (UF)	1919–1923
Howard Ferguson (C)	1923–1930
George Henry (C)	1930–1934
Mitchell Hepburn (L)	1934–1942
Gordon Conant (L)	1942–1943
H. C. Nixon (L)	1943
George Drew (PC)	1943–1948
Thomas Kennedy (PC)	1948–1949
Leslie Frost (PC)	1949–1961
John Robarts (PC)	1961–1971
William Davis (PC)	1971–

Macdonald

Mowat

Hepburn

Robarts

LAW AND ORDER

Court administration is traditionally the most confusing aspect of government in Ontario. New divisions have been created as required, and there have been few radical changes in judicial organization since the days of John Graves Simcoe.

But confusing as it seems, the judicial framework is not complicated. It consists of three main elements — the Supreme Court of Ontario, the chain of county and district courts, and the provincial courts. Each category is subdivided, but has carefully delineated responsibilities.

The Supreme Court of Ontario consists of twin divisions, the High Court of Justice and the Court of Appeal. The High Court tries major civil and criminal cases, with or without a jury. It is based in Toronto, but its justices regularly travel the province 'on circuit' to conduct the Assizes in each region.

Justices of the High Court are appointed by the federal government, as are justices of the Court of Appeal, where three, five, or seven judges sit together to rule on points of law. The Court of Appeal normally sits in Toronto, though it may occasionally visit an outside location, such as a penitentiary.

In the past, Supreme Court proceedings have been long and complicated and too expensive for many prospective litigants. But recent innovations have improved matters. Procedural changes and the introduction of 'pre-trial conferences' (at which adversaries define their differences) have saved time and expense when the case comes to court.

At the judiciary's middle level are the county and district courts, which are in the south and north of the province respectively. Each such court has civil and criminal jurisdiction. In civil matters, the court has jurisdiction in disputes involving sums up to $7500, and plaintiffs and defendants are represented by counsel.

Attached to the county and district courts are small-claims courts, which handle cases involving sums up to $400 (or $800 in some areas in the north) and where plaintiffs and defendants may represent themselves. In most areas the same judges preside, but in Toronto small-claims judges are separate.

Osgoode Hall in Toronto is the headquarters of the Law Society of Upper Canada, which administers the legal profession in Ontario.

Police

The Ontario Provincial Police is the third largest deployed force in North America, and the only provincial force in Canada besides Quebec's. It came into existence in 1909, following unprecedented lawlessness during the mining boom in Northern Ontario.

Today the OPP is responsible for policing rural areas, the provincial highway system, and also certain municipalities on a contract basis. Otherwise police work in municipalities is carried out by local agencies. The biggest is the Metropolitan Toronto force, which employs nearly a third of all police in the province.

Police personnel in Ontario's various agencies are trained at the Ontario Police College at Aylmer, near St. Thomas in Elgin county. The college aims to prepare police for all situations they will meet and claims that a trained officer is worth at least three untrained adversaries.

The Ontario Provincial Police are responsible for areas not covered by municipal forces. Among them is Georgian Bay, where provincial police patrol the many islands by launch.

provincial courts have a family division. They try cases involving juveniles and certain family matters, like subsistence following desertion (though the Supreme Court tries certain divorce matters, and the 'surrogate court,' part of the county or district court, handles adoptions).

Ontario's legal profession is administered by the Law Society of Upper Canada. Founded in 1797 at Newark (Niagara-on-the-Lake), the society is the oldest of its kind in North America. It has its headquarters at Osgoode Hall in Toronto (named for Upper Canada's first chief justice and Simcoe's chief ally, William Osgoode).

From the outset, all lawyers practising in Ontario were required to be members of the society. This meant joint membership of both barristers and solicitors, who in England participated in separate branches of the profession and were administered by separate bodies (as they still are). In Ontario, lawyers may fulfill both roles.

However, the tradition of separate branches lingers on. Though student lawyers take one set of final examinations, they must take separate oaths to be 'called to the bar' or 'admitted as solicitors.' From that point they may set up a practice, probably specializing in particular facets of the law, or join a partnership. Recent years have seen the emergence of specialist advocates who concentrate on court work.

At government level, four provincial departments fall under the 'justice secretariat.' These are the Ministries of the Attorney-General (chiefly concerned with courts and justice administration), the Solicitor-General (police matters), Correctional Services (penitentiaries, homes of detention), and Consumer and Commercial Affairs.

Ontario is divided into counties, each with its own court. The picturesque courthouse in Middlesex County in London, built in 1831, has been replaced by a modern structure.

For judicial purposes Southern Ontario is divided into 'counties,' and Northern Ontario is divided into 'districts.' ▼

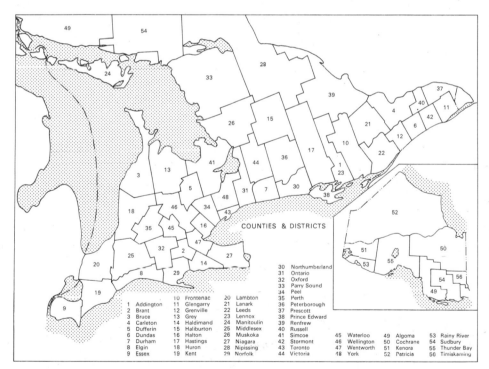

COUNTIES & DISTRICTS

		10 Frontenac	20 Lambton	30 Northumberland		
1 Addington	11 Glengarry	21 Lanark	31 Ontario		
2 Brant	12 Grenville	22 Leeds	32 Oxford		
3 Bruce	13 Grey	23 Lennox	33 Parry Sound		
4 Carleton	14 Haldimand	24 Manitoulin	34 Peel		
5 Dufferin	15 Haliburton	25 Middlesex	35 Perth		
6 Dundas	16 Halton	26 Muskoka	36 Peterborough	45 Waterloo	49 Algoma	53 Rainy River
7 Durham	17 Hastings	27 Niagara	37 Prescott	46 Wellington	50 Cochrane	54 Sudbury
8 Elgin	18 Huron	28 Nipissing	38 Prince Edward	47 Wentworth	51 Kenora	55 Thunder Bay
9 Essex	19 Kent	29 Norfolk	39 Renfrew	48 York	52 Patricia	56 Timiskaming
			40 Russell			

In criminal actions, county and district courts try cases of medium severity. The accused may elect to be tried with or without jury. If he chooses trial by jury, the proceedings are 'General Sessions of the Peace.' In both criminal and civil matters, there may be right of appeal to the Court of Appeal in the Supreme Court.

The provincial court tries petty criminal actions, and there may be right of appeal to the county or district court. The provincial court's judges — as opposed to federally appointed judges in county and district courts — are appointed by the province through the lieutenant-governor.

Besides their criminal jurisdiction,

SOCIAL SERVICES

A high proportion of Ontario's government spending goes to social services. Health and education each absorb about a quarter of the total, while social security and community services, including housing, claim a further 10 per cent.

The province's chief commitment in health matters is to operate the Ontario Health Insurance Plan (OHIP), available to all residents of Ontario who pay the necessary premium. The plan is designed to cover both physicians' fees for necessary medical services and hospital bills for necessary care and treatment.

Physicians' fees are determined by agreement between the Ontario Medical Association and the government, and the physicians are reimbursed for services provided. But public hospitals are usually granted a global sum to cover their operating costs each year, apart from additional income from semi-private and private rooms.

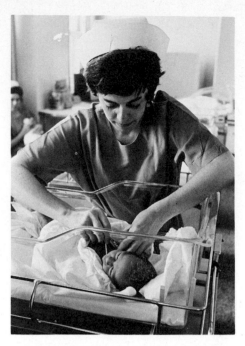

Certification of nursing staff is not mandatory in Ontario, but most hospitals prefer nurses and nursing assistants to have acquired local qualifications. There are some 90 000 registered nurses in Ontario, and some 30 000 registered nursing assistants.

There are nearly 250 public hospitals in Ontario, varying in size from the 1000-bed Toronto General to tiny cottage hospitals in remote communities. But nearly all are autonomous, non-profit corporations governed by a board of trustees. Most trustees are elected by those who have joined the corporation by paying a token fee.

In addition, the board includes a number of ex-officio members, including two or three representatives of the physicians permitted to admit patients to the hospital's facilities, and probably representatives of the body responsible for founding the hospital. In some cases this was the local municipality, in some a religious order.

The board appoints an executive director to administer all areas of the hospital's operations apart from the medical side, where the physicians and surgeons concerned are responsible directly to the board. Nursing staff, orderlies, and other workers are employed by

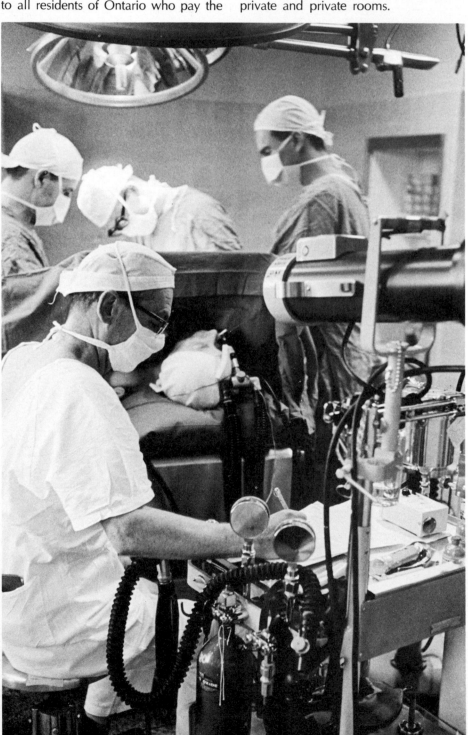

An operation in progress at a Toronto hospital. Nursing staff are employed by the hospital, but physicians and surgeons must apply for privileges from the hospital board before they may use its facilities. There are some 15 000 fully licensed MDs in Ontario.

Honours graduates at a Toronto high school receive their graduation diplomas.

reversed. Among its most controversial features was a bid to allow Ontario students free choice of subjects in high school. However this was not widely implemented and is being rescinded.

School attendance is compulsory from ages six to sixteen (though under provincial law it may be fourteen in certain rural areas). Many elementary schools offer voluntary kindergarten at age five, and then follow up to 12 or 13 grades or years in elementary and secondary schools. Grade 13 is an Ontario specialty introduced more than fifty years ago to prepare students for university.

Students may obtain secondary school graduation diplomas by gaining a minimum of twenty-seven credits (usually at the end of Grade 12). They may then move on to one of more than twenty colleges of applied arts and

technology (CAATs). With an extra six credits (subject to approval, and normally at the end of Grade 13), they may advance to university.

There are some fifteen publicly supported universities in Ontario. Longest established are the University of Toronto and Queen's University in Kingston. Others include Western Ontario (London), McMaster (Hamilton), York (Toronto), Guelph, Carleton (Ottawa), Trent (Peterborough), Brock (St. Catharines), Lakehead (Thunder Bay), and Windsor.

Social security programs cater to the elderly, handicapped, and financially needy. Old age homes and welfare funds are usually administered by the local authority concerned through funds granted by the province. Community service programs include adoption, child care, centres for the mentally retarded, and housing subsidies.

the hospital and fall under the executive director.

These arrangements hold in nearly all hospitals in the province, whether they are for 'active treatment' (the great majority), chronic, convalescent, or rehabilitation cases (for instance, after serious injury), or indeed nursing homes (where the province pays 90 per cent of fees). However, the province owns and operates all psychiatric hospitals.

As regards education, arrangements are quite different. The province has overall responsibility to provide free elementary and secondary education, but in practice delegates most of this to some 200 locally elected school boards. These assess the needs of the communities they serve, and in response build or repair schools and hire staff.

Where numbers justify it, Roman Catholic (and in two cases Protestant) minorities may organize a separate school board parallel to the local general school board. These may operate schools to Grade 10 level. However, Ontario does not support separate high schools with tax.

The arrangement is the result of considerable educational reform during the 1960s, much of which is now being

Trent University in Peterborough is one of the smallest universities in the province, but enjoys a beautiful location on the banks of the Trent Canal.

Franco-Ontarians

Some 500 000 Ontarians are of French descent, and of these 390 000 use French as their everyday language. The biggest concentrations are in the Ottawa valley and in the north-east. More are in the south-east, the Windsor area, and in Metropolitan Toronto.

Ontario is not by law a bilingual province, but in the educational field French schools are provided where the local school board (or separate school board) decides that they are needed. There are more than 300 French-language elementary schools, and 60 secondary schools — some completely French and some mixed, in that English and French share facilities.

At a tertiary level, there are French-language CAATs and two universities offering courses in French — the University of Ottawa and Laurentian University (Sudbury). In the health field, there have been moves to make more services available in French, both in hospitals and in the general health field.

Ontario initiated a French-language court in Sudbury in 1976, and subsequently established similar facilities in other centres in the north and the east. Ontarian civil servants are being encouraged to become bilingual, and ideally all government services will be available in both English and French throughout the province.

ARTS AND LETTERS

Before World War I when French impressionism was still the rage, a group of Toronto landscape artists was experimenting with a new concept in the wilds of Algonquin Park. They made design their priority and used colour to emphasize its form.

As it happened, most of them had been professional designers and had met while working in a graphic arts studio. Three were north-country Englishmen: J.E.H. MacDonald, Frederick Varley, and Arthur Lismer. The others were Canadian born, including Lawren Harris, A. Y. Jackson (who joined them only in 1912), and Tom Thomson.

During the war the friends went their own ways. Jackson and Varley served in Europe as official war artists. Lismer served in Canada. Thomson, largely self-taught but probably the most gifted of them all, was a woodsman at heart and continued painting in the Algonquins. In 1917 he drowned there in a mysterious canoe accident.

In 1919 most members of the 'Algonquin School' were back in Toronto, and with two new recruits they formed the 'Group of Seven,' pledged to continue the pioneering work already begun. The newcomers were Frank Johnston and Franklin Carmichael, though after the first exhibition Johnston dissociated himself and was later replaced by A. J. Casson.

All but one of the group were predominantly landscape painters. Varley preferred painting people, though later he too was converted. Two extra members, Edwin Holgate of Montreal and L. L. FitzGerald of Winnipeg, were coopted in 1931. But after a final exhibition in 1932, the group was disbanded.

Instead, its members founded a much larger organization — the Canadian Group of Painters, which aimed to encourage the growth of art throughout the nation. There were, in all, twenty-eight founding members drawn from across Canada, though most were from Ontario, and they and their successors

Arthur Lismer's *Bright Island*, **courtesy of the McMichael Canadian Collection, Kleinburg. Lismer was a lifelong teacher of art, active in South Africa and Australia, as well as Canada.**

exhibited regularly from 1933 until 1969.

The influence of the Canadian Group is clearly discernible today in the art of Ontario and the western provinces. For a long while its exhibitions were the only means by which Ontario's creative artists could make their work known. They created enough of a market to justify the emergence of commercial art galleries.

In the mid-1950s a group of abstract expressionists in Toronto decided to exhibit together as 'Painters Eleven' in a common bid to win recognition. They included Harold Town and Jack Bush, who went on to win international recognition, and together they wielded major influence on the shape of the arts in Canada.

In literature, Ontario's classic success has been Stephen Leacock. Brought up on a farm south of Lake Simcoe before the turn of the century, Leacock was appointed lecturer in political science at McGill University in Montreal. There he taught until his retirement in 1936, but he maintained a summer home in Orillia.

Leacock published many important books on economics and history, but he is remembered chiefly as a humourist — particularly for his sketches of 'Mariposa,' a fictional small town generally identified as Orillia. Leacock depicts himself as an informal raconteur, satirizing society through his cutting personal observations.

Leacock was buried in a church in Sutton, near Lake Simcoe. So is Mazo de la Roche, who between 1927 and 1960 wrote the sixteen Jalna romances. These are the chronicles of the fictional Whiteoaks family and their estate, Jalna, apparently set in the Oakville area west of Toronto. The books remain bestsellers in many languages.

In the late 1920s Morley Callaghan of Toronto was for a while a member of the American literary colony in Paris. He is best known for his short stories. Robertson Davies of Toronto, a playwright and a novelist, has been called Canada's leading man of letters. Margaret Laurence, Margaret Atwood of Toronto, and Alice Munro of Huronia have won wide respect for novels and short stories.

In the world of non-fiction, two figures from the University of Toronto have won acclaim — Donald Creighton in history and biography, and Marshal McLuhan in communications. There is a growing interest in poetry, particularly in Toronto, and public poetry readings by local poets attract enthusiastic response.

Pic Island (in Lake Superior) by Lawren Harris, courtesy of the McMichael Canadian Collection in Kleinburg. Harris was an original member of the Group of Seven and first president of the Canadian Group of Painters.

Mazo de la Roche

Stephen Leacock

Alice Munro

Robertson Davies

Donald Creighton

Morley Callaghan

Marshall McLuhan

Margaret Laurence

THE MEDIA

Canada has two national English-language television networks — CBC, which began broadcasting in 1952, and CTV, which commenced operations in 1960–61. Both concentrate their production facilities in Toronto.

CBC and CTV are keen rivals, and in Southern Ontario and British Columbia they face stiff competition from American stations across the border. Indeed, Toronto and Hamilton, with Canadian and American stations and special cable service, probably have a greater choice of television channels than anywhere else in the world.

Each network provides a full schedule of programs, whether for owned-and-operated stations (CBC has about fifteen across Canada) or for local affiliates. These are expected to carry certain obligatory programs and may run other available programs if they desire. Affiliates are paid an appropriate share of revenue for carrying network programs.

Productions from Toronto studios are beamed to other major centres in Canada by Anik communications satellite, then are distributed regionally by microwave landline. To co-ordinate timing in Canada's many zones, programs beamed from Toronto are 'taped and delayed' in Winnipeg, Regina, Alberta, and British Columbia, then are broadcast as scheduled.

Of course, 'tape and delay' is not possible in reverse. A special transmission of CBC's national news is beamed to the Maritimes an hour ahead of the live broadcast in Ontario. Certain 'live' broadcasts from Toronto are live only in the Maritimes and are taped and delayed even in Ontario.

Besides CBC and CTV, in addition Ontario has stations carrying the CBC French-language network, emanating chiefly from Montreal, and in some areas stations carrying the regional Global network, licensed in 1972. Since 1970 the Ontario Educational Communications Authority has run the provincial government's TV Ontario.

Inevitably, the success of television has greatly influenced the fate of radio. Throughout the 1960s it seemed that radio was to become nothing but background noise — whether classical music, pop, country and western, or whatever specialty the licensed station was committed to broadcast. All were paid for by commercials and, where appropriate, were beamed in stereo.

Instead, radio has made a strong comeback. In place of the old soap operas, which have now been conceded to television, radio listeners provide their own opera in the course of live phone-in debates. In similar fashion, the telephone has brought new immediacy to news reporting with in-depth interviewing of the personalities involved.

The CBC's English-language AM and FM services which, like television, are based in Toronto, have been largely responsible for the continuing success of radio. The radio services are entirely federally sponsored, and are expected to provide a wide variety of programs catering to all sectors of the population and not least to minorities.

Nearly all CBC English-language radio and television programs emanate from Toronto, while most French-language programs are broadcast from Montreal.

Daily newspapers have not held their own quite so well. The old habit of reading the newspaper every day is disappearing, and many readers see one only two or three times a week. Circulations have declined in spite of booming populations, but because of increased advertising revenue, newspapers are more profitable than ever.

In response, newspapers have tried to give the reading public what it says it wants — which is local news, dispensing with much of the strong national and international coverage once the hallmarks of Canadian journalism. The effect has tended to encourage greater provincialism and the acceptance of stereotype views of other regions.

The one exception in English-language journalism is the Toronto *Globe and Mail*, which has maintained general coverage in spite of ailing circulation. In contrast, the Toronto *Star* has easily the largest circulation in Canada, but concentrates on local politics, consumer and family affairs, and light entertainment.

Otherwise, Ontario's major newspapers include the Hamilton *Spectator*, the *London Free Press*, the Ottawa *Citizen*, and the *Toronto Sun*. There are, in all, nearly fifty dailies in Ontario, the majority of which are small-town operations sharing available readership with

Toronto papers circulated province-wide. Several dozen community weeklies cover only local news.

Nearly all the dailies are members of the Canadian Press, the national news co-operative. Some of its news is gathered by the agency's own staff, and international news is provided by other agencies on an exchange basis. But most of its material comes from the dailies themselves, and it is re-edited by the Canadian Press and submitted to its members.

Some newspapers have installed computerized equipment on which journalists can compose and correct their stories. The computer transmits them to an automatic type-setter.

Radio 'hot-line' and telephone current affairs programs have attracted a considerable listenership. Among the most successful has been CBC Radio's *As It Happens*, with Barbara Frum and Al Maitland (seated), and executive producer Robert Campbell.

PLAYS AND CONCERTS

In 1953, the little community of Stratford launched an ambitious 'Shakespearean Festival' — two plays staged in a marquee. The plays were so well received that the festival became an annual event, and today it is Canada's biggest and most prestigious.

The idea of the festival was suggested by Stratford's name, which had come about because the first building on the site had been the Shakespeare Inn, a roadhouse erected in the 1830s. Fortunately the city is set in charming surroundings on the Avon river, which has been a major factor in drawing enthusiasts to Stratford year after year.

Today the festival stages half a dozen Shakespearean plays each year, and in addition the works of other notables. They are performed in the handsome Festival Theatre, which has an open platform stage, and in other centres in the city. Also, there are concerts of orchestral and chamber music, folk, and jazz.

From fewer than 70 000 visitors in its first year, today the festival attracts more than 500 000. Its success is symptomatic of the progress of the performing arts throughout Canada, but particularly in Ontario, where there are more than forty professional theatre companies at work as well as scores of amateur groups.

Necessarily the chief focus of activity is Toronto, which possesses a string of professional theatres, each with its own company and an artistic director who sets a very personal stamp on its offerings. Important names are Toronto Arts Productions, Toronto Workshop Productions, Toronto Free Theatre, Factory Theatre Lab, Tarragon Theatre, and Theatre Passe Muraille.

Many actors are trained in the National Theatre School in Montreal or at university or community college, and are hired by theatre managements through the auspices of the stage actors' trade union, Canadian Equity. But an actor's career is not necessarily lucrative, and the vast majority have to supplement their stage earnings outside the theatre.

Worse still, Ontarians seem to resent local actors becoming stars — at least at home, though several have made big

names for themselves outside the country. As theatre prospers, however, this may change. Stratford and its younger counterpart, the Shaw Festival at Niagara-on-the-Lake, have raised standards to international levels.

There has been progress, too, both in opera and ballet. The Canadian Opera Company was founded in 1950 and performs in Toronto and Ottawa, besides making an annual national tour. Its home is Toronto's O'Keefe Centre.

Karen Kain, popular ballerina with the National Ballet of Canada, dances in a production of *Coppelia.* **She appears here with Jacques Gorrissen.**

An encouraging number of singers trained in Toronto have gone on to build international reputations.

Toronto's National Ballet of Canada was formed in 1950. Relying largely on talent developed in its ballet school, it is growing into one of the world's premier

The Hamilton Philharmonic Orchestra performs in the Great Hall of Hamilton Place.

The Stratford Festival Theatre makes 'theatre-in-the-round' possible, much as it appeared in Shakespeare's time.

The Toronto Mendelssohn Choir is probably Canada's longest-surviving musical organization.

companies. It is now nearly as well known in the United States as it is throughout Canada, but each year its most lavish season is reserved for Toronto.

In the music world, Ontario has more than thirty symphony orchestras, at least ten of which are wholly or partly professional. It has been the policy of the Ontario Arts Council to encourage decentralization of orchestras to break Toronto's cultural monopoly, and the result is a welcome proliferation throughout the province.

The best known orchestras are the fully professional Toronto Symphony, the Hamilton Philharmonic, and the National Arts, based in Ottawa. Pressing close on their heels are keen rivals in London, Kitchener-Waterloo, and St. Catharines. Each is based on a hard core of professionals, but includes a number of talented semi-professionals.

Each orchestra plays annual subscription and pop series in its home venue, as well as children's series and touring engagements throughout the province and sometimes outside. Funding is provided on the basis of one-third ticket sales and one-third grants, whether national, provincial, or municipal, and the remainder voluntary donation.

An important innovation in Ontario has been the annual Contact series organized for promising soloists. Representatives of orchestras throughout the country assemble to audition the soloists, and on the strength of their performance may book them for appearances.

Founded in 1894, the Toronto Mendelssohn Choir is probably Canada's longest-surviving musical organization. It consists of nearly 200 performers, among them the professional Festival Singers, who are Canada's most accomplished choral group. The remainder are amateurs who are expected to pass an annual audition in the interests of maintaining high standards.

SPORTS WORLD

Whatever the limitations in the stage and film world, Canada has no shortage of stars in its professional sports. Leading players of Canadian hockey, football, and baseball are heroes to millions and are paid salaries to match.

In the hockey world, the Toronto Maple Leafs have shared top billing with their arch-rivals, the Montreal Canadiens, for decades. The Leafs have been known as such since 1927, but the club was originally founded as St. Pats to take up a vacant franchise in the booming National Hockey League, which was founded in 1917.

The influence of the Leafs is felt throughout the province. Young boys (and not a few girls) dream of growing up to wear the Leafs' famous colours. Only a few succeed, but scores of others find their way into professional teams throughout North America, and represent one of Ontario's most impressive exports.

As regards Canadian football, Ontario has three of the four teams in the Canadian Football League's eastern conference — the Hamilton Tiger Cats,

the Ottawa Roughriders, and the Toronto Argonauts. Hamilton and Toronto have been football rivals since at least 1870, and it is supposed that they developed the game later adopted in the United States.

At the time of Confederation baseball was Canada's most popular sport, challenged only by the national game, lacrosse. Since then its career in Ontario has been checkered, though it has received steady support at the amateur level. In 1977, however, major league baseball returned to Toronto with the formation of the Blue Jays.

The professional teams receive the lion's share of attention from the media. But recent years have seen far more emphasis on participation by amateurs, partly through general interest in fitness, and partly through belated awareness of the fun involved and of the excitement of full-fledged competition.

Some of these amateur sports have been well supported for many years — for instance, golf, tennis, curling, and sailing. In such cases the accent is as much on the socializing involved as it is on the sport. The new emphasis concentrates more on really demanding physi-

cal activity, like swimming, athletics, gymnastics, and squash.

Amateur sport in Ontario blossomed visibly in response to the Montreal Olympics of 1976 — not least because Canadian competitors did not do as well as hoped. With the world's best on their doorstep, Canadians were given the chance to see what 'will to win' was all about.

There is no reason why Canadians should not do well in such competitions, as was shown by the swimmers at Montreal and by Canadian performances at several successive Winter Olympics. At least one Olympic sport was originated in Ontario — basketball, invented by James Naismith and his schoolmates of Almonte, using peach baskets as goals.

Later Naismith took his game to McGill University in Montreal, where he developed rules and eventually introduced the game at the YMCA in Springfield, Massachusetts, in 1891. But

Canadian football originated in Hamilton and Toronto and has remained a firm favourite in Ontario. Here the Toronto Argonauts press the Hamilton Tiger Cats.

as with lacrosse, which is another game developed largely in Ontario, local interest has waned and basketball today is played and supported by relatively few.

Amateur sports facilities involve heavy cash outlay, and much of the funding for tracks, courts, pools, and arenas is provided by various levels of government. In addition government provides a significant range of coaching services designed to improve standards, though some complain that they are restricted to top levels.

But the major responsibility for individual sports rests with the provincial and national associations formed to administer them. Ontario has more than seventy such associations, nearly all of which are members of Sport Ontario, which acts as spokesman for them and provides permanent offices for more than half at its headquarters in Toronto.

The typical provincial sports association is a federation of clubs throughout the province, and on their behalf it organizes competitions including a provincial championship. Most belong to appropriate national administrative bodies, some of which organize interprovincial championships.

In some sports the province is represented by its champion club team, and that is the Canadian tradition. More and more, however, provincial associations themselves select and coach a truly provincial team to reach appropriately higher standards. Such teams should help span the wide gap between local sport and international competition.

The stretch of Lake Ontario off Kingston offers some of Canada's finest sailing and was selected as the site of the 1976 Olympic sailing regatta.

Anglers build fishing huts on the ice of frozen lakes, cut a hole, and try their luck. The winter fishing season lasts from mid-January until the March thaw sets in. ▼

The Ontario Jockey Club organizes regular meets both in summer and winter. This is a meeting at Toronto's Woodbine racetrack.

generation. But the great majority have existed no more than a decade or two and are products of the great leisure boom which started in the 1950s.

Traditionally, cottages have been favoured by city-dwellers wanting to get away from it all. In many cases mothers and children like to spend all summer at the cottage, in which case fathers join them on weekends. Fortunately, roads to Southern Ontario's lake resorts have been greatly improved, and it is possible to commute.

In earlier days Ontario families bought remote lakefront plots from the provincial government, which was glad to dispose of otherwise useless land for a profit. However, the land's value is now so great that the government is no longer prepared to sell Crown land and when possible buys back land already alienated.

Instead, any available lakefront plots are leased subject to careful conditions. In Southern Ontario they have been so popular that no more are on offer, though there is less of a shortage farther north, where most of the lakes are situated. Freehold plots in the south change hands at high prices.

Most famous of the lake areas are Georgian Bay, in particular the Bruce area around Owen Sound and Collingwood, Huronia, around Barrie, and Muskoka, around Gravenhurst. Many

Though slopes are not as impressive as in some other provinces, skiing has become a major winter sport in Ontario. This is Tally Ho winter park near Huntsville in the Muskoka region.

LAKES AND MOUNTAINS

Nobody has counted Ontario's tens of thousands of lakes, much less named them all. But great numbers have been adopted by families who have built cottages beside them and, if possible, spend months and indeed whole summers in residence.

The lake cottage has become a key element in Ontarians' lifestyle. The idea of having a summer retreat is more than a century old, and many cottages have been handed down from generation to

The lakes of Northern Ontario are prime game-fishing grounds.

Moose hunting near Cochrane, Northern Ontario. A horn is used to reproduce a moose call and tempt the real animal from its hiding place.

Summer cottages dot the shore of Lake of the Woods, in Northern Ontario, near the Manitoba boundary.

cottages are accessible only by boat because they are on islands or because there is no road. In the north, areas near Sudbury, Sault Ste. Marie, and Thunder Bay are popular.

An old Ontario law that frustrates many cottage-owners is that some 22 m of land adjoining all navigable waterways, including lakes and rivers, is reserved to the Crown as 'road allowance' — a throwback to the needs of log drives in the heyday of the lumber industry. Cottages erected too close to the water are on Crown land.

Typical activities throughout the summer are fishing, sailing, canoeing, waterskiing, and, of course, just lazing in the sun. The same holds true of lake cottages in the north, though here families may prefer to keep themselves remote from neighbours, and, if possible, have a whole lake to themselves.

Originally most cottages were flimsily constructed, designed only for summer use. However, more and more have been winterized and are occupied throughout the year, owing to an increasing interest in winter sports. By lucky chance the prime lake country of Bruce, Huronia, and Muskoka is also first-rate ski territory.

Cross-country skiing in these areas and elsewhere has seen a great upsurge in recent years. Downhill skiing is organized at a number of attractive resorts. Centres are equipped with chairlifts and ski tows to carry skiers to the tops of the slopes, and with fine hotels for the *après-ski* set.

Besides the skiing, winter cottagers enjoy skating on frozen lakes and probably some winter fishing through holes cut in the ice. Lake country is crisscrossed by special snowmobile trails,

just as in summer it is laced by hiking and canoe routes, which encourage Ontarians to seek out their pioneer origins.

Not everybody likes to be limited to one location, though in Ontario 'the lake' and 'the cottage' are terms with special personal meanings for tens of thousands. Instead, many opt for a camper to explore the wilderness, or a yacht to cruise around islands in the lakes, or a motor-cruiser to explore Ontario's inland waterways.

Two of these waterways are particularly attractive, both canal systems which long ago outlived their original purposes. One is the Rideau Canal, between Ottawa and Kingston, which makes extensive use of the Rideau river and lakes. The other is the Trent–Severn waterway, linking Lake Ontario with Georgian Bay by way of Peterborough and Orillia.

THE INDIANS

Ontario has a greater diversity of 'Indians' than anywhere else on earth. They include blacks from the Caribbean, and East Indians from India proper and other locations in Asia, East and South Africa, and even the West Indies.

Each of these groups embraces a variety of languages, dialects, and cultures. But none of the groups is as diverse as Ontario's 'native Indians,' including both true indigenous peoples who inhabited the region before the arrival of white men, and other Indian groups who entered the area subsequently.

Today Ontario's native Indians are scattered at intervals throughout the province, with the greatest concentration in Toronto, which has an estimated Indian population of more than 20 000. Otherwise, most registered Indians live in or near white settlements or on one of several dozen 'reserves' administered by the federal government.

In general terms there are four Indian cultural divisions, distinguished by common history and traditions that characterize their way of life. One is the Algonquian-speaking peoples in the eastern half of the province; another is the Iroquoian-speaking groups living in the south-west and near Kingston.

The third, the great majority of Ontario's Indians, is the Cree. Most are in the north-west. The fourth, the Ojibwa, are found in all parts of the province. Some Ojibwa have been settled in Ontario for centuries, while others have arrived more recently from the west, or like the Iroquois, from the south.

The province's Indians have maintained a relatively low profile in recent decades, and many Ontarians have not been aware of their presence. Traditional policy has aimed to 'civilize' them in whatever ways possible, by obliging children to attend school, where they will hopefully absorb enough 'white' ideas to play a part in society.

The program has not been a success. Too often schools have been staffed by middle-class, English-speaking teachers without any understanding of the very different world in which Indian children have been raised. Apart form the communication problem — fewer than half the children speak any English — they

A victim's eye view of a Cree hunter in the making.

find that Indians reject outside notions of discipline.

The majority of Indian children drop out of school long before progressing far enough to gain much benefit from it. The few who persevere and eventually reach university are drawn mostly from the south — those in closest contact with whites. Even then they find the system disillusioning, because it takes no account of them as Indians.

Ironically, it has been the experience of coping with new Canadians from alien cultures that has encouraged both federal and provincial educationists to change their concepts of Indian education. Both have recognized the virtues of educating Indians as Indians, and not as stereotypes of white culture.

The federal government's Indian education program, however, remains conservative — a matter of teaching Indian languages and beadwork. In contrast, Ontario's provincial program aims to include special curricula for Indian schools, incorporating the history of the tribes and — just as important — their folklore.

In some instances, the history affects Indians' dealings with whites. These include the part played by Indians in defending Canada against American invaders in the War of 1812, and, sub-

Lacrosse remains Canada's official national game, though its profile is low compared with its popularity in earlier days. Lacrosse sticks are manufactured by Indians in a factory near Cornwall.

sequently, alongside British regulars and the Canadian militia. Indians can take as much pride in their victories as white Canadians can in theirs.

But just as interesting and indeed exciting is the history of Indian peoples' dealings with one another. Examples are the wars between tribes of the Iroquois confederation and the Ojibwa of the north, with all Central Ontario as their battleground. Indian history goes back centuries before any white men appeared on the scene.

Folklore is something different — a series of moralistic stories which, to the Indian, are as important (not to say sacred) as Bible stories are to Christians. Many of the stories were used by Henry Wadsworth Longfellow in his Hiawatha poems, though he garbled them and drew them from the traditions of several different peoples.

A major painting school has emerged among Ojibwa Indians of the woodlands of north-western Ontario, chiefly through the work of Norval Morisseau.

One positive effect of the reawakening of Indian consciousness is that it benefits not Indians alone, but all Canadians. It teaches them that there are other views of the history of their country and its people — new dimensions which will help them appreciate its very special character and particularly its native heritage.

Manitoulin Island in Georgian Bay, the world's largest freshwater island, has long been sacred to the Indians of central Canada and particularly to the Cree and Ojibwa. It is the home of 'great spirits,' both good and bad.

PARKS AND WILDLIFE

In the mid-nineteenth century, loggers of the Ottawa valley reached mighty stands of white pine on the Algonquin uplands. For decades they felled trees without interruption, but in 1893 the provincial government declared the vast area a natural reserve.

The decision was a landmark, but it was not made to save trees. The loggers felled pines as before and soon absorbed hardwoods farther west. Instead, the idea was to preserve the region as a natural wildlife habitat — which meant keeping out would-be settlers and encouraging loggers to take more care.

Algonquin Park today is 7653 km² in extent. In over 75 per cent of it, logging continues as in the old days, but so selectively that few visitors notice. Natural regeneration means that the forest's annual growth compensates for the harvest, and special care is taken to preserve the aesthetics of roads, lakes, and nature trails.

In sheer size and grandeur, Algonquin Park is in a class by itself. But in the years since its creation, the province has opened more than 120 provincial parks. All but one have come into being since the mid-1950s — the period which marked the start of the great leisure boom.

The parks are grouped in five categories. The great majority are either 'recreation parks' or 'natural environment parks,' and like Algonquin, each is carefully maintained and most are equipped with modern camping facilities. The difference between the two groups is that 'natural environment' means what it says.

There are eight 'nature reserves' protecting areas of special scientific interest, five 'wild river parks' provided for canoeists, and most interesting of all, three 'wilderness parks.' One of these, Quetico near the Manitoba border, is a paradise of more than 1000 lakes and waterways abutting a similar area in Minnesota.

Besides the provincial parks, Ontario has three national parks. They are tiny but are of special interest, since they preserve unique flora and fauna: the 'islands' parks in the St. Lawrence and Georgian Bay, established in 1904 and 1929 respectively, and the Point Pelée park (1918), on Lake Erie at Canada's southernmost tip.

All natural wildlife in Ontario belongs to the Crown, whether it is in or out of the parks or 'wildlife management areas' reserved by the province. Each species and every area is monitored to make sure that wildlife balance is maintained. Except in designated areas, surplus game is culled by licenced hunters in a declared 'open season.'

Balance, in fact, was the original point of wildlife management. However, with increasing concern for the environment, it has been extended to cover all species, and not least those in danger of extinction. Ontario has four species classed as endangered — timber rattlesnake, blue racer snake, bald eagle, and peregrine falcon.

Moose are normally timid and make themselves scarce when a stranger happens upon them.

Fortunately most other species are thriving. The beaver population is, indeed, far too great, though more are harvested by trappers than at the height of the fur trade. Beavers remain a favourite of visitors to provincial parks, as do moose, white-tailed deer, and black bears.

These are animals typical of Ontario's hinterland. More unusual are the species found in the southern tip — particularly songbirds found nowhere else in Canada, and a number of amphibians and reptiles. The Bruce Peninsula in Georgian Bay is Ontario's last great natural sanctuary south of the Canadian Shield.

But potentially most interesting of all is the great Polar Bear Park on Hudson Bay and James Bay, at present accessi-

Park wardens are available in most provincial parks to explain local flora and fauna to visitors.

ble only by air or by water. As yet the park attracts only a handful of visitors, but its 24 000 km² is the untouched habitat of polar bear, caribou, wolf, walrus, seal, and a host of other animals.

A formation of Canada geese migrating south for the winter skims the Great Lakes.

Many parks contain a big beaver population, which may be quickly located through the remarkable dams that the beavers construct.

THE ENVIRONMENT

Increases in population and industrial activity have taken a heavy toll on Ontario's environment. Belatedly, the public conscience has been stirred to do something about pollution, whether of water, air, or land.

Basically, pollution occurs when a product is added to the environment in quantities that adversely affect nature's ability to dispose of it. This product may be natural, but most of the trouble comes from man-made pollution. Included in the category is a good deal of 'nuisance' pollution, like noise and smell.

More serious, however, is the pollution that directly affects the life cycle. Each element in nature is closely related to neighbouring elements, and this is particularly the case in the food chain. A plant relies on sunlight and water; an animal eats the plant; man eats the animal. Pollution in the water or air will affect the man.

The pollution that first attracted public notice in Ontario was of water — most obvious in Lakes Erie and Ontario. For a century these have been natural dumping grounds for industrial and municipal waste from the communities that surround them, whether in Ontario or the United States.

The waste has two principal effects, both harmful. On the one hand, some materials decompose and use up oxygen, leaving appreciably less for the fish to breathe. On the other — and paradoxically — some are nutritious and encourage uncontrollable plant growth. This provides extra food for fish species which may be less desirable.

Besides these, many toxic pollutants from industry, agriculture, and municipal sewage have reached Ontario's waters. One of the most serious of these is methyl mercury. This is a form of soluble mercury discharged from certain chemical plants. It enters fish through their skins and gills, and so infiltrates the food chain.

Already mercury pollution — some of it natural — has affected inland waters in many regions of the province, contaminating fish and endangering the lives of local Indians and others with regular fish diets. However, industrial concerns utilizing mercury cells are now

obliged to contain them or shut down their operations.

The second major category of pollution is in the air, whether caused by gas or by particles. One major gaseous pollutant is sulphuric oxide, produced by burning coal or oil (as in power stations) or through petroleum refining, some pulp and paper operations, and sulphide ore smelting. Another is carbon monoxide.

Carbon monoxide is produced when fossil fuels are burned where there is a shortage of oxygen. The worst offender is the automobile, particularly in confined urban areas. However, automobile manufacturers have taken steps to improve combustion of gasoline so that more of it is used up and less is discharged as exhaust.

Ontario's environmental beauty is one of the province's most valuable resources and is carefully protected by government agencies for the benefit of all.

Carbon monoxide is harmful to people and animals, but the automobile's exhaust also produces nitrogen and hydrocarbons. These are harmless in themselves, but in combination they may be affected by sunlight and can form 'ozone' or 'petrochemical fog,' which is harmful to plants. Again manufacturers have taken action.

The third category is land pollution. This is generally less harmful to health but is bad for morale. It takes the form of abuse of the landscape — whether by urban development, industrialization, forestry or mining, through litter or solid

waste in general, or even by the siting of transport routes and power lines.

In this connection, mining and forestry companies have been under concerted attack from Southern Ontario. In response, some have made great efforts to improve matters. Where trees were felled wholesale, there is now conscientious reforestation, and mining companies are expected to rehabilitate land which they have affected.

The environmental movement has had a short life but has had some notable successes — a tribute to the power of collective action. The public at large, government, and ultimately the industries concerned have all played parts. Inevitably the processes used mean that production is more expensive. But few complain.

A major contributor to air pollution is south-western Ontario's large population of automobiles.

Winter and summer, inspectors of the Ministry of the Environment test lakes and rivers for pollution. ▼

In the nickel mines of Sudbury, waste water from the mine is purified deep underground before it is pumped to the surface for release into natural watercourses.

The spectacle of Niagara Falls makes it Ontario's leading tourist attraction.

Downstream from the falls, an aerial car carries tourists to view a major whirlpool.

NIAGARA

Between Lakes Erie and Ontario runs the Niagara river, 56 km long and the sole drainage channel for the northern Great Lakes. The river negotiates the Niagara Escarpment, then plunges in a dizzying leap which forms Ontario's greatest tourist attraction.

Geologists estimate that the Falls originated about 25 000 years ago, in the age of the Wisconsin glacier. Originally they were situated in the neighbourhood of Queenston Heights, but since then they have eaten their way some 11 km back into the rock. On the Canadian side the drop is about 54 m.

Currently the river is divided by Goat Island, which separates the American Falls from the more spectacular Horseshoe Falls on the Ontario side. Both have been major draws since early in the nineteenth century and used to inspire wild and astonishing stunts. Many are commemorated in a museum nearby.

These stunts included the antics of the Great Blondin, a noted French acrobat and tightrope walker. In 1859 he several times crossed a guyed wire suspended over the Falls. Once he walked with his feet in pails; another time he took out a stove and fried an egg; on yet another he turned somersaults and swung hand over hand.

The climax of his performances came when he crossed with his manager on his shoulders. Three times the manager, Harry Colcord, had to disembark at guy ropes so that Blondin could rest. But they completed the journey and did so on two subsequent occasions before Colcord decided that he had had enough.

Photograph Credits

Abitibi Paper: (Gilbert A. Milne & Co., Ltd.) p. 32 bottom, p. 33, (Lockwood Survey Corp., Ltd.) p. 32 top; *Archives Nationales du Quebec*: (GH 1072-144) p. 17 bottom left; *Art Gallery of Ontario*: p. 78 top; *Canada Dept. of Indian & Northern Affairs*: p. 88 bottom, p. 89 top; *Canada Packers*: p. 50 top, p. 51 top, (C. Vella) p. 50 bottom; *Canadian National*: p. 57 bottom right and centre, p. 66 top; *CBC*: p. 80, (Harold White Photography) p. 81 top; *City of St. Catharines*: (Port Weller Dry Docks Ltd.) p. 49 bottom left; *Humphry Clinker*: p. 15 top right, p. 55 top right, p. 65 top, p. 67 bottom right, p. 68 bottom left, p. 71 bottom left, p. 74 top, p. 81 top, p. 85 bottom right; *Dofasco*: p. 44 bottom; *Domtar Chemicals*: (Graetz Bros.) p. 37 bottom; *Dupont of Canada*: (Douglas Paisley Studio) p. 48; *Eastern Construction*: (Panda Associates Photography and Art Services) p. 53 top and bottom; *Ford of Canada*: p. 46 bottom; *General Foods*: (Ron Vickers Ltd.) p. 51 bottom; *General Motors of Canada*: p. 46 top, p. 47 top; *Hamilton Place*: p. 83 top; *Imperial Oil*: p. 21 top; *Inco*: p. 39 bottom, p. 93 bottom right; *Labour Council of Metropolitan Toronto*: p. 54, p. 55 left; *Macmillan of Canada Ltd.*: p. 79 third row right and left, second row right; *McGraw-Hill Ryerson Ltd.*: (Victor Aziz) p. 79 second row left; *Massey-Ferguson*: p. 18; *Metropolitan To-ronto Library Board*: p. 11 centre, p. 16, p. 17 top, p. 79 top left and right; *National Ballet of Canada*: p. 82; *Noranda Mines*: p. 36 bottom, p. 40, p. 41 top right, p. 43, (Feature Four Ltd.) p. 20 top, p. 42 top, p. 43; *NorOntair*: p. 57 bottom left; *Northern Telecom*: p. 21 bottom left; *Ontario Archives*: (S2145) p. 11 bottom centre, (S1072) p. 11 bottom right, (144C) p. 11 bottom left, (S4758) p. 15 top left, (S13290) p. 22 bottom, (S307) p. 73 top left, (L733) p. 73 top right, (S323) p. 73 bottom left, (S14174) p. 73 bottom right; *Ontario Hospital Assoc.*: (James H. Peacock) p. 76 top right and bottom left; *Ontario Hydro*: (BR6611) p. 60 top, (J1190A) p. 60 bottom, (2A6156) p. 61 bottom right, (BR6312) p. 61 bottom left; *Ontario Ministry of Agriculture & Food*: (68-2445) p. 20 bottom, (75-B302) p. 22 bottom right, (75-B2) p. 23 centre, (74-B427) p. 23 bottom, (72-B183) p. 23 top, (721-1887) p. 24, (5B-22-4) p. 25 bottom, (72-3353) p. 25 top right, (72-3241) p. 26 bottom, (69-B292) p. 27 top, (66-914) p. 28, (66-B176) p. 27 top, (66-914) p. 28, (72-3241) p. 15 top right, (66-693) p. 29 bottom left, (72-3269) p. 29 top left; *Ontario Ministry of the Environment*: p. 3, p. 93 top and bottom left; *Ontario Ministry of Industry & Tourism*: p. 4 top, p. 6, p. 7 top right and bottom left, p. 9 top and bottom left, p. 10 top, p. 12, p. 19 top left and right and bottom, p. 35 top, p. 37 top right, p. 41 bottom, p. 45 top and bottom, p. 52, p. 56, p. 58 bottom, p. 59 bottom right and left, p. 62 top and bottom, p. 63 top and bottom, p. 64, p. 67 left and right, p. 68 top, p. 69 top and bottom, p. 70, p. 71 top, p. 73 top left, p. 75 top, p. 77 bottom, p. 83 bottom, p. 84, p. 85 top and bottom left, p. 86 top and bottom, p. 87 top and bottom, p. 90, p. 92, p. 94 top and bottom; *Ontario Ministry of Natural Resources*: p. 4 bottom, p. 5 bottom right, p. 7 bottom right, p. 30, p. 31 top left, bottom left, and centre, p. 34 top and bottom, p. 35 bottom, p. 88 top, p. 91 top right and bottom; *Ontario Parks Branch*: p. 91 top left; *Ontario Provincial Police*: p. 74 bottom; *The McMichael Canadian Collection*: p. 78 bottom, p. 79 bottom left; *Rio Algom*: (Frank Grant, G/W Photography Ltd.) p. 37 top left; *Royal Bank of Canada*: p. 65 bottom; *The Seaway*: p. 58 top; *Donn Silvis*: p. 66 bottom; *Eedie Steiner*: p. 79 bottom right; *Stelco*: p. 44 top; *Stratford Shakespearean Festival*: (Robert Ragsdale, A.R.P.S.) p. 83 centre; *Texasgulf*: (Herbert Nott & Co., Ltd.) p. 42 bottom; *Union Carbide of Canada*: (James C. Fish Photography) p. 49 bottom right; *University of Toronto, Centre for Culture and Technology*: p. 79 bottom centre; *Westinghouse Canada*: p. 49 top left.

Acknowledgments

Many individuals, corporations, institutions, and government departments assisted us in gathering information and illustrations. Among them we owe special thanks to the following:

Abitibi Paper Company
Automotive Parts Manufacturers Association
Board of Trade of Metropolitan Toronto
CHIN Radio
Cadillac Fairview
Canada Packers
Canadian Association in Support of the Native Peoples
Canadian Bankers Association
Canadian Broadcasting Corporation
Canadian Conference on the Arts
Canadian Copper and Brass Development Association
Canadian Daily Newspaper Publishers Association
Canadian Equity
Canadian Hospital Association
Canadian Life Insurance Association
Canadian Manufacturers Association
Canadian National
Carleton University
City of Hamilton
City of Kingston
City of Ottawa
City of St. Catharines
City of Thunder Bay
City of Toronto
City of Windsor
Conference Board in Canada
Dominion Foundries and Steel
Domtar Chemicals
Eastern Construction
Ford Motor Company of Canada

General Motors of Canada
General Foods
Geological Survey of Canada
The *Globe and Mail*
Imperial Oil
Inco Limited
International Caravan
Labour Council of Metropolitan Toronto
Massey–Ferguson
McMichael Canadian Collection
Motor Vehicle Manufacturers Association
National Ballet of Canada
National Hockey League
Noranda Mines
Northern Telecom
Ontario Archives
Ontario Arts Council
Ontario Chamber of Commerce
Ontario Council of Wine
Ontario Federation of Agriculture
Ontario Federation of Labour
Ontario Forest Industries Association
Ontario Hydro
Ontario Ministry of Agriculture and Food
Ontario Ministry of Colleges and Universities
Ontario Ministry of Culture and Recreation
Ontario Ministry of Education
Ontario Ministry of Health
Ontario Ministry of Industry and Tourism
Ontario Ministry of Labour

Ontario Ministry of Natural Resources
Ontario Ministry of Revenue
Ontario Ministry of Transportation and Communications
Ontario Ministry of Treasury Economics and Intergovernmental Affairs
Ontario Ministry of the Attorney-General
Ontario Ministry of the Environment
Ontario Mining Association
Ontario Northland
Ontario Police Commission
Public Archives of Canada
The Seaway
Shaw Festival
Sport Ontario
Statistics Canada
Stelco Limited
Stratford Shakespearean Festival
Supreme Court of Ontario
Toronto Argonauts
Toronto Public Library
Toronto Stock Exchange
Toronto Transit Commission
Union of Ontario Indians
University of Ottawa
University of Toronto
Union Carbide Canada
Westinghouse Canada
Zinc Institute, Inc.

Canadian Cataloguing in Publication Data

Hocking, Anthony, 1944-
    Ontario

(Canada series)

Includes index.
ISBN 0-07-082692-7

1. Ontario.   2. Ontario—Description and travel.
I. Series.

FC3061.6.H63   971.3   C77-001599-9
F1057.5.H63

1 2 3 4 5 6 7 8 9 0   BP   7 6 5 4 3 2 1 0 9 8

Printed and bound in Canada

Index